The Culture and Civilization of Pakistan

The Culture and Civilization of Pakistan

Kishwar Naheed

Translated by

Amina Azfar

THE **PLATINUM** SERIES

OXFORD
UNIVERSITY PRESS

OXFORD
UNIVERSITY PRESS

Oxford University Press is a department of the University of Oxford.
It furthers the University's objective of excellence in research, scholarship,
and education by publishing worldwide. Oxford is a registered trade mark of
Oxford University Press in the UK and in certain other countries

Published in Pakistan by
Ameena Saiyid, Oxford University Press
No.38, Sector 15, Korangi Industrial Area,
PO Box 8214, Karachi-74900, Pakistan

ISBN 978-0-19-940773-6

Typeset in Adobe Garamond Pro
Printed on 70gsm Offset Paper

Printed by Le Topical Pvt. Ltd, Lahore

Acknowledgements

Cover Image: Lok Virsa Museum, Islamabad

Contents

Prologue

MY MOTHER GAVE BIRTH TO ME IN BULAND SHEHR AT THE time when the Pakistan Resolution was being passed in Lahore. The hardships of the Second World War, rationing, high-heeled shoes worn by the British, processions of men and women chanting '*Lai ke rahengae Pakistan*' (We will have Pakistan, we will!), slogans shouted by us children, picking up sticks with which we played *gulli danda* in the streets every evening, and setting out in processions; these images—like Sheherzade's Arabian Nights of kidnapped girls and murdered boys in every lane—stayed with us. Such was my childhood.

After the birth of Pakistan, the arrival of strangers and encountering new accents became familiar very soon because children of my age used to narrate gory episodes to each other in timid, hushed voices when our elders' backs were turned.

It was such episodes that turned life into a fearful reality from youth to old age. I spent fifteen years observing the roughly built homes of the deprived and talking to the elderly of my own age. Fahmida Riyaz, Ameena Saiyid, and Umair Lodhi insisted on my setting down on paper all that I had seen. Moreover, my grown-up children asserted that they had never known their compatriots to speak the truth.

I do not claim that only what I have written is true; however what is now before you is all the truth I have seen and read. History and geography are not taught in our country. What I am writing has been extracted from many books after prodding the memories of many friends, especially I.A. Rehman and Ashfaque Saleem Mirza, who delved into their own childhood to enlighten me. Perchance this book will become a vindication for my life and for future generations, a strong reference point for the past.

Kishwar Naheed

1

Introduction: From the Formation of Pakistan to its Division

WHEN I TURN THE LEAVES OF HISTORY, I FIND THAT THE BILL for the partition of the subcontinent approved by the British Parliament on 15 July 1947 was passed by the House of Lords on 16 July, and became an Act on 18 July 1947. It is known as the Indian Independence Act 1947. Lord Mountbatten suggested that both India and Pakistan announce their independence on 15 August. Quaid-e-Azam Mohammad Ali Jinnah disagreed; and so King George VI gave his consent both to the announcement of Pakistan's independence on 14 March, and Quaid-e-Azam's assumption of power as the Governor General. Pakistan's Dominion Status continued until 1956 and ended with the passing and coming into effect of the Constitution of Pakistan, when the state was declared the Democratic Republic of Pakistan. On 17 August 1947, the Radcliffe Award determined the boundaries of India and Pakistan. Radcliffe was in a hurry to leave the subcontinent. In keeping with the dividing line he had drawn, Gurdaspur should have come to Pakistan, but at Lord Mountbatten's persuasion it was made a part of India because it afforded India its only land route to Kashmir. Jinnah accepted this apportionment after much argument, calling his new country a 'moth-eaten

1

Pakistan'. West Pakistan now comprised Muslim majority areas of Balochistan, the North-West Frontier Province, Punjab, and Sindh, while East Pakistan encompassed the Muslim majority areas of Bengal. Together, the East and the West wings became the state of Pakistan.

On the first of August 1947, Muslim government servants were given the option of staying in India or moving to Pakistan. Special trains were allocated to carry those who had opted for Pakistan from New Delhi to Karachi since Karachi was then the capital of Pakistan.

On arrival in Pakistan these people were given small government quarters to live in. But their offices were bereft of chairs and tables; acacia thorns were used to keep papers together. However, the spirit of the new arrivals was young. It is an historical fact that when on the seventh of August 1947 a small Dakota plane brought Quaid-e-Azam from Delhi to Karachi, all the roads were chock-a-block with enthusiastic crowds. All eyes were glued to the plane from which the Quaid was about to emerge. Then came the moment when Quaid-e-Azam, dressed in a white sherwani, with a Jinnah hat over his head and accompanied by Mohtarma Fatima Jinnah, made his appearance. Shouts of '*Quaid-e-Azam Zindabad*' rising from all sides rent the air. Women who had crowded the roofs of nearby houses had joined in the slogan chanting. Then came the night, between 13 and 14 August when Mustafa Ali Hamdani's voice resonated with the proclamation: 'This is Radio Pakistan, Lahore'. Trains carrying government employees were also transporting their families. Since these convoys of passengers were travelling under government protection, they were not subjected to massacres. Besides these, the early trains carrying migrants from Meerut and Lucknow also arrived safely in Lahore.

Lahore was a sizeable trade centre where business was in the hands of the Hindus. The railways employed a large part of the Muslim population. Hindus lived in new suburbs like Model Town and Krishan Nagar as well as in the inner city. Most Hindu families locked up their houses and left for Amritsar thinking they would return once the carnage was over. Riding the waves of emotions, slogans turned into flames. On the other side, massacres of Muslims and abductions of Muslim girls on trains leaving India for Pakistan continued for many months. Under the Nehru-Liaquat agreement, the Khokrapar route had been opened. In 1948, the Lahore border had been left open for only the families of government servants to enter through. Within this period of a year and a half, hundreds of thousands of Muslims, Hindus and Sikhs lost their lives and thousands of young girls were abducted. Some of the abducted girls were found by their families. Among the unfortunate rest who stayed alive, the Sikh girls converted to Islam and the Muslim girls became Hindus or Sikhs and remained in India under their Hindu or Sikh names. Many heart-rending short stories were written on these gruesome events on both sides of the border. The poetess Amrita Pritam wrote:

Today I say to Waris Shah,
Speak from within the grave
And open up another page
Of the Chronicle of Love.

There wept a Daughter of Punjab
You wrote and kept on writing.
                    (Translated by Salman Tariq Kureshi)

Pakistan had been divided into East and West Pakistan. Thousands of Indian miles lying between the two wings of the country, their two different languages, and then the untimely announcement by Quaid-e-Azam that Urdu alone could be the national language for the whole country, altogether precipitated violence over the language issue (which ended in the 1971 division of the country into Bangladesh and Pakistan). In 1955 West Pakistan was made 'One Unit', merging all its four provinces into one.

The One Unit was dissolved in 1971 and West Pakistan, now Pakistan, reverted to its earlier form of four provinces: Khyber Pakhtunkhwa, Balochistan, Sind, and Punjab. While Balochistan has the largest area, Punjab is the most populous. Sindhi is spoken in most of Sind. Many languages are spoken in Karachi which is the largest city of Sind and Pakistan. They are Sindhi, Urdu, Punjabi, Gujrati, Pashto, and English. The diverse communities who live in Karachi—Aga Khanis, Parsees, Bohris—speak their own languages as well as English and Urdu.

Balochistan is populated by Balochs, Pashtuns, and Punjabis. The languages spoken in this province are Brahvi, Balochi, Punjabi, and Pashto. Likewise, Punjabi, Siraiki, Potohari, and Hindko are spoken in Punjab. Urdu is the language of education and is spoken all over the country including the 'Tribal Areas'. Gilgit and Hunza have twenty-two local languages but Urdu is spoken and understood everywhere. Kashmiri, Dogri, and Punjabi are spoken in Azad Kashmir but Urdu is commonly spoken and understood throughout this area as well.

Besides its obvious utility in communication, a language is also savoured for its bouquet and flavour which it acquires in certain environments. In the rural areas and small towns of Punjab and also in the villages and provincial towns of the rest of Pakistan, people gather in the evening to listen to age-old tales, folk or Sufi poetry such as Heer Waris Shah, Shah Husain, Khwaja Ghulam Farid, or Shah Latif. It is remarkable that most of these rural audiences were uneducated and even illiterate, yet generation after generation this oral tradition endured. A hookah was placed in the centre of the assemblage and its pipe went from one person to another, while the sequence of recitation continued, round after round. The midnight hour would be long past before people retired to their homes.

All around the city of Lahore were gardens where people would sit in groups, listening to sagas or discussing politics while children played all around them. Late in the evening, the elderly would leave for their homes while the young would stay behind and have themselves massaged, sometimes just their hair, and sometimes full bodies with oil. The fashion for massage spread in Lahore. In Huzoori Bagh, the garden in front of the Badshahi Masjid, masseurs could be seen sauntering around, waiting for clients. In Lahore's city centre, people would be sitting by the roadside, chatting. The reason was that they came from small houses where they lived in joint families. There was no custom of husbands and wives conversing with each other; only every year a new child would arrive.

Lahore's Kashmiri Bazaar was famous for its books and storytelling. Every evening story writers would read out stories in an engaging style and voice. The stories had titles like 'Look, the airplane approaches' (*Dekho Jahaz Aya*), 'Ride the train' (*Karo Savari Rail Guddi Ki*), and, 'The Story of Heer and Ranjha' (*Qissa Heer Ranjhae ka*). These four-page stories would sell for two annas each. Our respected seniors Dr Faqir Husain Faqir and Ehsaan Danish used to sell booklets with collections of their verse in this way.

The whole of Shah Alam Bazaar was set on fire during the partition riots. Many of the shops in Anarkali were also torched. Only one shop remained undamaged which belonged to a Muslim. It continued to do business for a long time after Partition.

Most of the people who came from East Punjab travelled to Faisalabad, Multan, Bahawalpur, Khaniwal and Sahiwal in central Punjab, either because they had family there or because these places offered the kind of commerce which the newcomers were used to in the region they had left.

In Sind some of the Hindu and Sikh business families crossed the border from Khokrapar. Others travelled to India via Lahore. Many Memons, and the Adamji and Haroon families who had helped in the creation of Pakistan with their money and hard work, stayed in the new country. Parsi families too did not leave. The Aga Khan had helped the Quaid significantly in the creation of Pakistan. Aga Khani and Bohri families along with Christians remained in Pakistan. Hindu tribes living in places in interior Sind like Thatta, Sukkhar, Tharparkar, Badin, and Hyderabad did not move to India. However, in the last two decades, many Hindus have migrated to India as a result of the upsurge of religious orthodoxy. Even at the time of Partition, most of Sind's industrial establishments were located in Karachi. Interior Sind boasted only two or three cement factories, railway workshops, rice mills and small scale industries which were involved in the leather business. Unjust distribution of urban and rural evacuee property in Sind left behind by Hindus, caused ill feeling. At first altogether 7,850,000 refugees from India entered Punjab, Sind, Balochistan, and the Frontier province (Khyber Pakhtoonkhwa). About 1,00,000 Hindus left Sind, to be replaced by 2,000,000 Muslims from India. In 1961, this figure was further increased. 600,000 displaced persons from East Punjab also headed for Sind. The truth is that in the distribution of evacuee property, the poor Sindhi *hari* or peasant, as well as the helpless and indigent refugee working man were equally deprived. In the resulting conflict it was this very disadvantaged class that had to take the brunt of its fallout. Nationalistic Sindhi journalists highlighted these issues, and a detailed assessment was made in the Sind Hari Report.

Historically, the valley of Sind has always been a multilingual region. Even before the Aryans, the arrival of the Dravidians influenced the local dialects. Scholars of Sindhi have agreed that history has imposed few changes on the form of the Sindhi language which was at first written in the ancient Nagari script and later in the Arabic script. Wacholi is spoken in central Sind and Thari in Tharparkar. Kachhi and Gujrati are spoken in lower Sind, and the Lassi accent is heard in Lasbella.

The population in some parts of Sind has a Baloch majority but the Baloch accent, language, and the Baloch society are not considered apart from the stream of the collective Sindhi society. Similarly the Makrani and Shidi cultures also are absorbed in the Sindhi civilization.

Political activities in Sind are carried on under many different names. The Jeay Sind Tehreek was founded for Sindhi rights. The Baloch Students' Federation and Punjabi-Pakhtoon Ittehad were formed for similar ends. However, Sindhi groups did not advance in those days.

Before the birth of Pakistan, more than half the area of Balochistan came under British administration. Balochistan was divided into British Balochistan and the area that came under the princely states. British Balochistan consisted of the Murri, Bugti areas, and those tribal areas through which the railway line and military highways passed, linking the subcontinent to Afghanistan and Iran. Qalat, Lasbela, Kharan and Makran comprised the princely states of Balochistan. Quaid-e-Azam made his first contact with Balochistan on 29 March 1947 when he emphasized the implementation of political, economic, and educational reforms, and imposition of the Fourteen Points. On 14 August 1947 when the question of Balochistan's joining Pakistan arose, a royal jirga was instituted and the resolution for merging with Pakistan was passed with the concurrence of the majority. But despite the merger with Pakistan, the tribal system continued. Court cases are still decided through jirgas. On 14 February 1948, Quaid-e-Azam distributed robes of honour (*khilat*) to the sardars. At the behest of Qazi Issa, political workers were given statuses equal to those of tribal chiefs.

Forty-five per cent of the area of Balochistan is hilly, while fifty-five per cent is uneven land. Among all the provinces of Pakistan, Balochistan's population is the smallest. Its eastern region which consists of Katchi, Sibbi, and Naseerabad, is a vast plain. Balochistan is known all over the world for its excellent fruits including dried fruits. Apples growing on trees planted along the roads give out a wonderful fragrance. Almond trees can be seen in many places and the 150 varieties of dates grown in Balochistan are quite famous.

After Partition, radio stations were set up, first in Quetta, and then in Khuzdar, Turbat, and Zhob. In Quetta there is a television centre as well which televises programmes in Balochi, Pashto, and Brahvi. A publication in Balochi and Pashto published initially by the department of Information is now published under the Federal Department of Publications. In the field of education there are, in addition to the Balochistan University, a Women's University and a Cadet College. Balochistan University offers co-education and so does the Balochistan Arts Council. The Sibi Mela, an event where cattle shows, industrial exhibitions, and *mushairas* are held, is famous all over the country.

A whole goat, roasted on an open fire is widely eaten in the winter by tribal chiefs. The *sajji* is now popular all over the country and is made from lamb as well as chicken. In Chaman, a whole lamb sprinkled with salt is cooked in sealed pots buried in the ground. Natives and tourists alike enjoy eating it with leavened bread. For the last twenty years, women wrapped in chadors can be seen accompanying their men to restaurants. Rural women are rarely seen in the bazaars even now. Only older women in Baloch garb can be observed doing their grocery shopping.

In the last thirty years, owing to the arrival of the Afghan refugees, the blue, white and black burqas worn by Afghan women have become popular among Baloch women. Afghan embroidery is different from Baloch embroidery. Afghan refugees have tent settlements all over Balochistan. The Afghan refugees' culture has made inroads into the daily lives of the Baloch and the Pashtuns as well as Punjabi settlers. Many madrasas have been established to provide religious education. Baloch women and even little girls wear indigenous Baloch clothing, which is embroidered, has an open dupatta, a kurta that looks like a frock, and a pyjama with embroidery on the lower edges of both its legs. This outfit is popular in urban as well as rural areas, though the shalwar, kameez, and dupatta outfit is becoming common thanks to the school uniforms which consist of those three items.

The Baloch outfit for men includes a loose shalwar with wide legs, a long kameez, a waistcoat with Baloch embroidery, and a turban made of three to five yards of fabric. Like the Peshawar sandals, the Baloch slippers for men are embroidered in the local style. Sheep and goats raised in villages feed on wild shrubs.

Happy events used to be celebrated by firing guns. The weapon of choice now widely used for rejoicing is the Kalashnikov.

Mutual conflicts among tribes often result in bloodshed. Marriage outside one's tribe is uncommon. Wedding expenses are borne entirely by the man. Efforts are being made to do away with the custom of marrying within the family, as this often results in children with thalassemia—a disease which is almost untreatable. Women in every village of the Kech district earn good money from preparing heavily embroidered ensembles for women of Baloch families resident in Qatar and Amman.

Ziarat is a scenic spot in Balochistan where Quaid-e-Azam spent some time at the end of his life. Ziarat is famous for two reasons. One is that the juniper trees present in jungles are five to seven thousand years old, in areas around it. The United Nations has declared these forests the second 'living fossils' of the world. The second reason for Ziarat's fame is the presence of the Ziarat Residency there, which was burnt down by terrorists on 15 June 2013. Only the Quaid's room remained undamaged by the conflagration. Expert engineers rebuilt the residency. Even today, numerous tourists and schoolchildren visit the last abode of the Quaid every day.

At the very outset, there was a conflict in Pakistan between Ghaffar Khan's Red Shirts and the Muslim League. The former wanted independence while the latter were for inclusion of the area in Pakistan. Finally it was decided that the issue would be settled by holding a referendum. The majority voted for Pakistan and the area became a part of Pakistan. Subsequently, most of the Hindus and Sikhs left for India by way of Lahore. Some Sikh families went to Afghanistan. The Red Shirts remained, albeit peacefully, in Mardan and Swabi. Khan Abdul Qayuum Khan led the Frontier government after Dr Khan. Between the Frontier Province and Afghanistan ran the Durand Line which went down to Balochistan. This 'line' had been created by the British and was to last a hundred years, i.e. from 1893 to 1993. Even though Pakistan has created a border at Landikotal and Chaman and the people who take this route require a visa, the border is long and it is not possible to erect a barbed wire fence or armed posts all along it. Consequently, Pashtuns and Afghans sometimes cross illegally into Quetta from Qandahar and sometimes from Peshawar into Jalalabad or Kabul. The governments of Pakistan and Afghanistan have not dealt seriously with this situation. More importantly, smuggling between these areas, which was thriving even before the establishment of Pakistan and continued subsequently, has not been fully controlled.

Before the birth of Pakistan, Kabul was a dream destination just as Dubai used to be for Pakistanis thirty years ago. Stories mothers told their children would end with the triumphant hero bringing a bride from Kabul. The Qissa Khwani Bazaar in Peshawar was, as its name suggests, famous for its storytellers. People would roast potatoes on a skillet while they listened to the tales. Women attending a wedding or any other celebration would carry with them a live hen or eggs grasped under an arm. Everywhere, whether it was Charsadda or Mardan, Frontier women used to cover themselves with a chador. But after the arrival of the Afghans thirty years ago, the blue Afghan burka began to come into evidence. However, all Pathans are known for their habit of taking snuff and eating mutton. Orange pulao, *aloo gosht* and *naan*, sweet wheat bread flavoured with fennel and cardamom, and more than all these, the *chapli* kebab, were part of their everyday fare.

East Bengal as East Pakistan used to be a part of Pakistan until 1971. But Dacca could never become the capital of Pakistan. Because of the conflict with the army and the bureaucracy, the people of East Pakistan decided to establish a country of their own. On 16 December 1971, General Niazi surrendered to the Indian army chief, and a third new country, Bangladesh, was created in the subcontinent. Subsequently, famous Bengali artistes, such as Shahnaz Begum, Firdausi Begum, Runa Laila, Basheer Ahmed, and Rehman left for Bangladesh. Pakistan and Bangladesh have not been able to forge a strong, friendly relationship to date because the capacity of the Bengali hearts has shrunk owing to the harsh stages the people of East Pakistan had to pass after the birth of Pakistan. They teach these things in their courses of education and repeat them on the media. Faiz Ahmed Faiz was part of the delegation which accompanied Zulfikar Ali Bhutto to Bangladesh shortly after the emergence of the country. He wrote his impressions of what he observed there in the following:

Khoon ke dhabbai dhulenge kitni barsaton ke baad

How many more monsoons will go by before the bloodstains are washed clean

Before the emergence of Bangladesh the colour of the Pakistani passport was light green and was inscribed with the words 'Pakistan' in English, Urdu, and Bengali. In 1974, after the split, the cover of the passport became dark green and carried the words, 'Islami Jamhuriya Pakistan'.

2
Our Literary Scenario

A FTER THE ESTABLISHMENT OF PAKISTAN, BETWEEN 1947 AND 1952, most stories and poetry were linked to memories of the bloodsheds that had divided families. Women were dishonoured and thousands of them were abducted. In those days leaders of the Progressive Movement in literature, Syed Sajjad Zaheer, Syed Sibte Hasan, Hasan Nasir, and Faiz Ahmed Faiz were in Pakistan. Faiz Ahmed Faiz wrote about this scenario:

> *Yeh dagh dagh ujala yeh shab guzeeda seher*
> *Woh intezar tha jis ka, yeh woh seher toh naheen*

> This mottled light, this night-bitten dawn
> Surely this is not the much-awaited morn

Saadat Hasan Manto wrote short stories like *Khol do* and *Toba Tek Singh*. The American publishing house Maktaba-e-Franklin asked Manto to translate these for them, offering to pay him well for the translation. In response Manto wrote *Letters to Uncle Sam*, in which he describes the mad scramble of the post-Partition scene in Pakistan. Qudratullah Shahab depicted a similar scenario in his *Ya Khuda*. An extremely complicated social crisis was created as a result of the changes in culture

15

and severance of families. Earlier every family knew the background of their distant relatives; now all individuals [and their backgrounds] were mixed up, as Quratul Ain has written in her *Housing Society* and *Sita Hiran*. The immigrant Sindhi, Sita Mir Chandani, and much more her old mother, recall their lost paradise. They are nostalgic about the roads, streets, and temples of Karachi. Intezar Husain wrote *Gali, Koochae, Kankarian*, and more than that the novel in which the wound of separation from East Pakistan is exposed—*Basti*. Abdullah Husain wrote the story of southern Punjab from 1930 to 1947 in his *Udas Naslain*.

Before these writers came on the scene, Urdu literature was going through a phase of aesthetic and romantic writing. The desire for freedom and democracy was widespread. Iqbal and Shibli Nomani showed the way for national and communal movements. Subsequently, poets, especially ones like Hasrat Mohani, Chakbast, Zafar Ali Khan, and Josh created enthusiasm for the struggle for freedom. Meanwhile Maulvi Mumtaz Ali started a movement for the awakening of women. The Progressive Movement was initiated in this period; impassioned songs were written on the dignity of labour. Dr Rasheed Jahan compiled *Angaray*, a collection of short stories, which made vested interests squirm. They put pressure on the government and had it proscribed. Yet the Progressive Movement remained unhurt in Pakistan. In India Majaz wrote:

Tu is aanchal say aik parcham bana leti toh achcha tha

You should have made a flag out of your dupatta.

And in Pakistan Faiz Ahmed Faiz wrote:

Bol, keh lub azaad hain tairay

Speak, for your lips are free.

Ahmed Nadeem Qasmi published *Naqoosh* with Hajra Masroor.
Later, he published and edited *Funoon*, stopping only when
he died. Conservatism had put down strong roots in Pakistan,
and arrests were made under the Rawalpindi Conspiracy Case
which included Major General Akbar Khan and Faiz Ahmed
Faiz. Other members of the Progressive Movement, including
Syed Sajjad Zaheer and Sibte Hasan went underground. Hasan
Nasir who was related to the royal family of Hyderabad was also
involved in the struggle for revolution and change in Pakistan.
The police arrested him and shut him up in the infamous cell at
Shahi Qila, where ultimately he was tortured to death. Hameed
Akhter wrote about this torture cell under the title of *Kal Kothri*
[Black Hole]. Later, Salahuddin Haider also wrote a detailed
account of the torture inflicted in this prison of the fortress.

From Pakistan, Syed Sajjad Zaheer relocated to India where
Pandit Nehru received him in the country with much honour.
Quratul Ain Haider also relocated to India after writing a great
novel like *Aag ka Darya* because conservative newspapers were
relentlessly critical of her. Taking advantage of the political
chaos in Pakistan, Ayub Khan took over the government. In
1964 when general elections were announced, Miss Fatima
Jinnah came forward to challenge him and was supported by
the Jamaat-e-Islami amongst others. A revolutionary poet who

we now remember by the name of Habib Jalib now arrived on the scene. Just before Miss Jinnah's speeches he would recite his latest poem which referred to a current issue, for example:

Bees rupiya mun aata
Is par bhi hai sunnata
Gohar, Sehgal, Adamji
Banai hain Birla aur Tata
Mulk kai dushman kehlatay hain
Jub hum kartay hain faryad
Sadder Ayub Zindabad

Wheat flour, at twenty rupees per maund
Yet there is a dead silence
Gohar, Sehgal, Adamji
Have turned into Birla and Tata
We are called enemies of the State
When we cry out
President Ayub, Zindabad!

Ayub Khan won the elections using the government's machinery, even though Habib Jalib went around reading everywhere:

Aisay dustoor ko, subh-e-baynoor ko
Mein naheen manta, mein naheen manta

To this kind of system, an unlit dawn,
I do not acquiesce, I do not submit

Such poetry caused governments to incarcerate him. But as soon as he was released he would write more poetry that fired up the nation all over again. This was comparable to what happened in the case of Faiz: When Faiz was in jail, his latest poetry—*ghazal* or *nazam*—would somehow be smuggled out. Copies would then be made of it and distributed all over the country.

Jalib flew his own banner even during Benazir's time in power. He wrote:

> *Har Bilawal hai des ka maqrooz*
> *Paoon nungay hain Benaziron kai*

> Every Bilawal is in debt to the State
> Unshod are the feet of all Benazirs

Revolutionary poetry was at its peak in the days of Zia ul-Haq, when no sooner was a sentence pronounced on persons (of even between the ages of 11 and 40 years), it was carried out, and the prisoner whipped within half an hour. Thus the tone of every poet became revolutionary. Saleem Shahid has said:

> *Qaid meray jism kay undur koiee wehshe na ho*
> *Saans laita hoon toh aati hai sada zanjeer ki*

> Could there be a savage imprisoned in my body
> For when I breathe I hear the sound of chains

Fahmida Riaz had to be present in court every day. Finally, she left for India. This exceptional poet of femininity only returned to Pakistan seven years later when she received an invitation for Benazir's wedding. As long as Benazir's government lasted, Fahmida had a job. The day the government ended, she was out of a job. Ahmed Faraz wrote about the tragedy of writers unconscionably attending a meeting called by Zia ul-Haq in his poem *Muhasira*. First he was forced to leave Sind, then, accepting exile he remained outside Pakistan for six years. To protect Faiz Ahmed Faiz from a similar indignity, Palestinian leader, Yasser Arafat invited him to Lebanon where he was appointed Editor of *Lotus*, a literary journal of the Middle East.

Among women writers, Nisar Aziz Butt wrote a novel *Nay Chiraghae Nay Gulay* about the Pakistan Movement in Pakhtunkhwa. Khadija Mastoor wrote her novel, *Angan,* about the Pakistan Movement in U.P. Jameela Hashmi wrote *Aatish-e-Rafta* in which she recounted the riots in both East and West Punjab. Hajra Masroor and Khatija Mastoor wrote the stories of women made homeless and destroyed by the riots. In a book on Ashfaq Ahmed's life, Banu Qudsia wrote about refugees in Walton. Bapsi Siddhwa also wrote an account of the refugees as well as abduction of young girls in her novel, *Zaitoon*. Similarly Altaf Fatima, Farkhanda Lodhi, Zaitoon Bano, Khairunnissa Jafri, Mussarat Kalanchwi, and Raffat Noor-ul-Huda Shah wrote in Urdu and other languages of the country, the sufferings of our women and their fortitude in living their lives despite them.

Masood Mufti, Ummeh Amara, Masood Ashar, and Abdullah Husain described movingly the tragedy of the separation of East Pakistan. For the last thirty years the themes of terrorism in Pakistan, the attacks on mosques, temples, and churches have dominated short stories and novels. Mustansar Husain

Tarar, Hameed Shahid, Nilofer Iqbal, Tahira Iqbal, Munsha Yaad, Rasheed Amjad, Anwar Sajjad, Mazharul Islam, Ahmed Dawood, and Aijaz Rahi have presented in their works—in addition to the days of the Zia ul-Haq regime—the atmosphere of terrorism in such a way that one is reminded of the atrocities committed by the Nazis. Khalida Husain is the most respected writer among all of these, and Asif Farrukhi has earned much fame for his stories and editorial work.

At the time of the creation of Pakistan another class of novels became famous. These highlighted the reign of the Abbasids and Muslim rulers of Spain. Novelists like Naseem Hijazi, M. Aslam, Rasheed Akhter Nadvi became very popular. Then came the next generation of writers, like Intezar Husain and Mumtaz Mufti, whose style greatly influenced their successors.

Akhtar Shirani is identified and invoked by the romantic genre of Urdu poetry. Meeraji, Thasadduq Husain Khalid, Noon Meem Rashid, Majeed Amjad, and Mukhtar Siddiqui, created new pathways in the genre of the *nazam*. Faiz Ahmed Faiz gave these a tone that is still popular. After the *nazam*, came the prose poem. The influence of Western poetry and conditions in Pakistan is apparent in the poetry of Iftikhar Jalib, Qamar Jameel, Abdur Rasheed, Sara Shagufta, Tanveer Anjum, and Anees Nagi. Concurrently, the feminist tone began to be recognized and Fahmida Riaz, Fatma Hasan, Yasmeen Hameed and Azra Abbas's style of writing became popular. The new tone in *nazam* was adopted by poets like Afzaal Syed, Zeeshan Sahil, and Dr Wahid. References to the deteriorating state of affairs in Pakistan are found in the works of all senior and contemporary poets. However, Zafar Iqbal and Muneer Niazi introduced a different style.

In Punjabi, Dr Faqeer Husain wrote poetry and also brought out a periodical. Najam Hussain Syed and Ahmed Rahi wrote in the vein of classical poetry. Afzal Hasan Randhawa and Fakhar Zaman wrote novels, while Nasreen Anjum Bhatti and Mushtaq Soofi's *nazams* are a manifestation of Punjab's culture.

Siraiki is spoken in the area stretching from southern Punjab to Bahawalpur. Everybody remembers the names of Rafat Abbas, Kaifi Jampuri, Arshad Multani, Nasrullah Nasir, Irshad Kalanchwi, and Ashiq Bozdar. Najam Husain Syed, Abbas Athhar, and Shafqat Tanveer Mirza represent freedom of thought in Punjabi poetry. In Punjabi prose, Farkhanda Lodhi and Afzal Tauseef show the mirror to the poison in the environment. Nisar Usmani, Minhaj Barna, and Zamir Niazi tried to unchain journalism. Anwar Ali Almaruf Nunha, Jawed Iqbal, Rafiq Feica, and Yousuf Lodhi Al Maruf Vai El showed a picture of society in their works.

I have not referred to the folk and classical literature of Punjab. Who in the subcontinent doesn't know Shah Husain, Sultan Bahu, Waris Shah, Baba Farid, Ghulam Fareed, Bulleh Shah, and the writer of Saif-ul-Malook, Mian Mohammad Bakhsh? Similarly, the *tappa*, *mahia*, *geet*, are popular in every village and city.

In the Balochi language the name of Must Tawakkali is known everywhere. Gul Khan Naseer and Ata Shad were revolutionary poets who wrote in Balochi as well. Shah Mohammad Murri has written biographies of numerous Baloch freedom leaders. The flow of folk poetry mirrors the work of the local labourers and peasants. Folk poetry passes down as oral tradition from one generation to the next and under which, even the names of the folk poets are often unfamiliar. In this genre, descriptions of the birth of a child, of marriage, sorrows, laments, separations and death flow in waves of emotions.

Folk songs and classical writings can be found in Brahvi as well as in Balochi. In 1955 the modern Brahvi short story made its debut. Mir Haibat Khan, Gul Mungal Zai, Ghulam Nabi Rahi, Hamida Nasreen and Shaheena Anjum head the list of names in this connection. In 1982 the first collection of short stories by Taj Raisani was published. The works of all Balochi and Brahvi writers of our day portray cultural anguish, political conflict, and moral degeneration. Sindhi, Urdu, and Balochi words are found in Brahvi short stories. Classical Russian short stories and novels are being translated in Brahvi while wedding songs can be found in all the languages of the country.

Coming to the Sindhi language, we find that Shah Latif's poetry is popular in every town and village. By combining classical and folk poetries, Shaikh Ayaz reached the summit of popularity in this genre. G.M. Syed and Dr Nabi Bakhsh Baloch wrote the history of Sind. A whiff of feminism reached here too. Seher Imdad, Atiya Dawood, and Amar Sindhu are new poets who exposed the true nature of the Sindhi *vadera*. Even after the creation of Pakistan, the landowners, and *vaderas* of Sind were so powerful that peasants living on their property could never breathe freely.

Sind's first great personality of the nineteenth century was Hasan Ali Afandi who was born in the year 1830. Despite the fact that he came from a poor family in Hyderabad, his love of knowledge was such that in 1885 he was able to establish the Sind Madrasatul Islam in a small building opposite Bolton Market. This institution is now a university. Afandi collected donations for it not only from the length and breadth of Sind but also from the states of Junagarh, Bhopal, and Hyderabad Deccan. Hindus and Parsis of this era also helped in the advancement of education in Sind.

After the fall of East Pakistan, one hundred and fifty thousand refugees came to Karachi. In the same period Punjabi and Pathan settlers also arrived in Sind especially in Karachi. The result was a nightmarish economic, social and organizational crisis which kept proliferating. But Comrade Abdul Qadir, Sobhogayan Chandani and Abdul Majeed Sindi—great sons of Sind—remained linked to the Hari (peasant) Movement.

In 1961, the capital of Pakistan had been shifted from Karachi to Islamabad. It was followed by a drop in the importance of Karachi. In the same period Naseem Kharal, Amar Jaleel, Agha Saleem, Murad Ali Mirza, and Mumtaz Mirza created a new image of Karachi and Sindh. Agha Saleem, Hasan Mujtaba, and Afaaq Siddiqi translated *Shah jo Risalo*.

The same period saw the rise of the memoir. Pir Ali Mohammad

Rashdi, Lutfullah Khan, Sobhogayan Chandani and Gopal Das Khosla are famous in this connection. Renowned contributions to Urdu writing are Shaukat Siddiqi's *Khuda ki Basti*, Dr Ahsan Faruqi's *Sangam*, Mumtaz Shirin's *Apni Nagarya*, Mohammad Khalid Akhter's *Chakiwara main Wissal*, Hasan Manzar's *25 Shumal 67 Mashriq* and *Maripur*, and Asad Mohammad Khan's *Toofaan*. An objective reality can be seen breathing in these stories. In the works of Ghulam Abbas, Syed Mohammad Anwar, Sagheer Malal, Hameed Kashmiri, Saeeda Gazdar, and Zahida Hina can be seen the far-flung locale of Sind and unidealized localities of Tharparkar.

In the soul of the Frontier Province, now known as KPK (Khyber Pakhtunkhwa), are reflected Rahman Baba and Khushhal Khan Khatak. Later, Ghani Khan wrote poetry and painted, but published very little of his work in poetry. Some people made a collection of his poems and published it posthumously. The Afghanistan-KPK frontier is spread over hundreds of miles. Thousands of Afghans cross the KPK and Balochistan-Afghanistan border in either direction every day. This has been going on for many years and men and women have been freely travelling back and forth, causing worry to the governments of Pakistan and Afghanistan. An attempt was made to destroy the tomb of Rehman Baba in a bomb blast. Bacha Khan University was attacked killing more than 22 students. Pakistani poets, especially those from KPK have made this and related topics themes for their poetry. A famous name in the history of KPK is Amir Hamza Shunwari. Ajmal Khan Khatak writes both poetry and prose very well. Among women writers, Zaitoon Bano is known for her short stories and Taj

Sayeed's name is important in the areas of editing and writing poetry. A familiar name among contemporary poets is Gulrez Tabassum. The environment of KPK has been deeply affected by the arrival of Afghan refugees, extremism, and radicalism. Young writers are, however, writing about a new horizon and peace in the world.

3

Our Fine Arts—On the National and International Planes

WHEN PAKISTAN CAME INTO BEING, USTAD SHARIF USED TO write numbers on train carriages. Later, he used the iconic stories of Heer Ranjha to depict the Punjabi culture. Ustad Sharif was the first to portray the landscape of Punjab. Before Partition, Amrita Shergil's was a familiar name among those who painted great paintings. Ustad Allah Bakhsh was also a renowned artist of this period. He too was a skilled landscape painter. He taught art at the National College of Arts until the end of his life. In 1963, he was awarded the Pride of Performance.

In Pakistan the leading name in water colour and Moghul style painting is of Abdur Rehman Chughtai. He gave a new aspect to Ghalib's couplets in his art. When Shakir Ali came to Pakistan after studying art in JJ School of Art and Slade School in London, he popularized abstract art. Ali Imam, Shimza, and Zubeida Agha furthered this new form of art, each in his/her own way. A department of Fine Arts was founded in the Punjab University. It was headed by Anna Molka Ahmed. She too chose the genre of landscape painting as her domain. Mural painting was still unknown when Sadequain painted the first mural in

Mangla Dam, which was combined with calligraphy. After he returned from France, Sadequain adopted calligraphy. His 'painterly calligraphy' appears on the ceiling of the Museum at Lahore as well as in numerous mosques and museums in India and Pakistan.

In abstract painting, Zahoorul Huq and Guljee opened new paths for younger artists. Zubeida Agha, and after her Saleema Hashmi, Naheed Raza, Meher Afroze and later women artists, linked the figure of woman with minutiae of the image now associated with *chador and chardivari*, or the woman in cultural/religious seclusion. Khalid Iqbal and Ghulam Rasool painted landscapes, and Qudoos Mirza gave the message that the human being has been turned into a puppet in the present age. Shazia Sikander, Rashid Rana, and Imran Quraishi's contributions to the installation genre of art have been acknowledged internationally. Jamil Naqsh's woman and pigeon became a symbol of freedom. Pakistani artists have not only exhibited their paintings internationally but have also gained a prominent presence in installation art. Furthermore, Hanif Ramay and Shimza also introduced individualism to their calligraphy. Aftab Zafar's work in calligraphy and painting is realistic. His work on calendars and diaries is unmatched. Shakeel Siddiqi has been extremely creative in realistic art.

In classical music, Ustad Barrai Ghulam Ali Khan left for India after Partition. Roshanara Begum is the jewel of our culture of music. Thanks to Ustad Amanat Ali Khan and Fatah Ali Khan, as well as Ustad Salamat Ali Khan and Nazakat Ali Khan, Pakistan's classical singing was credited with authentic merit all over the world, even in the early days of the country. Fareeda Khanum, Iqbal Bano, and Zahida Parveen, made a departure from Begum Akhtar's style in rendering *thumri, dadra,* and classical singing of the *ghazal.* Among later *ghazal* singers Shahida Parveen, Bilqees Khanum, Rubina Bader, Naheed Akhter, Runa Laila, and Mehnaz sang *ghazals, geets* and *naghmas* very well. The great Mehdi Hasan made his mark in *ghazal* singing and none could rival him in either Pakistan or India. Ghulam Ali was another excellent *ghazal* singer but could not match Mehdi Hasan's style. Abida Parveen had a distinctive style in singing *ghazal* and folk songs. Zahida Perveen and Pathanae Khan became much acclaimed singers of *kafi.* In Sind, Allun Faqir and Mohammad Yousuf rose to heights of the art in singing folk songs. The names of Ustad Sharif Khan Poonchwalae and later his son Arshad Shareef stand out as *sitar* players. Arshad Shareef now lives in Germany where he trains young people and also works on polishing his own talent. Ustad Shaukat is renowned as a tabla player and Ustad Nazim as a *sarangi* player. There are very few *sarangi* players nowadays. Ajmal's name is important as a tabla player. Ustad Salamat Ali is a flute player of distinction and Raees Khan is an important *sitar* player. Ustad Fateh Ali Khan was deaf and used to play the *sitar* with its string in his mouth. His son Ustad Nafees Khan is a skilled *sitar* player. In Karachi, Ustad Bundoo Khan and after him Ustad Umrao Bandoo Khan became renowned for playing the *sarangi.*

In the genre of the qawwali, Ghulam Fareed Sabri, Bakhshi Salamat, Meher Ali Sher Ali and Amjad Sabri had made their mark, but Nusrat Fateh Ali brought fame to not only the qawwali but also his homeland, Pakistan. His name is inscribed in the Guinness Book of World Records. Along with him, the qawwali singer Aziz Mian also made a name for himself. His son Imran Aziz has a repertoire of classical Persian and Urdu works in his memory bag. Qawwali singer Munshi Raziuddin is saturated with Arabic, Persian, and Urdu, (especially Amir Khusro's) melodies. Now his son Fareed Ayaz and with him, Abu Mohammad are earning a name for themselves.

In folk music, Alam Lohar, Ataullah Isakhelvi, Suraiya Multanikar, and Tufail Niazi have made their mark. Actually Tufail Niazi and Alam Lohar used to sing in public fairs. With the arrival of television, their fame and popularity grew. Nowadays Saain Zahoor who used to sing in old Anarkali has acquired world fame and made his own group. In the early period of Pakistan, Saain Marna's single-stringed instrument called *iktara* became famous. Faiz Baloch from Balochistan and Allan Faqir and Maai Bhagi from Sind also made the grade. Khamiso Khan, also from Sind, made his name in playing the *alghoza*. Inayat Hasan Bhatti and Bali Jatti sang well in fairs and festivals. Inayat Hasan Bhatti later worked in movies. Malka Pukhraj and subsequently her daughter Tahira Saiyid won worldwide fame in singing *ghazals* and *dogri* songs from Kashmir and Jammu. The genre of folk singing has never produced a singer who could equal Reshman.

Munir Sarhadi and Bakhtiar Sarwar became famous in KPK for their proficiency in playing the *sarinda*. In singing Punjabi folk songs, especially Shah Husain, Hamid Ali Bela was unrivalled. When Bela could not earn enough from his singing, he would turn to whitewashing houses. This alternate occupation ruined his throat. Even though Ustad Badruz Zaman, Qamaruz Zaman, as well as Imtiaz Ali and Riaz Ali learned classical singing and even sang in the genre, they could not earn the fame that came to Ghulam Hasan Shaggan.

Among the new generation of singers, the names of Asad Amanat Ali Khan (deceased), Rafaqat Ali Khan, Hamid Ali Khan, Shafqat Ali Khan, Ali Zafar, Atif Aslam, and Freeha Pervaiz are prominent. Noorjahan and after her, Naseem Begum and Zubaida Khanum contributed many memorable songs to the genre of film songs. Prominent among the early singers of Pakistan were Inayat Husain Bhatti, Saleem Raza, Munir Husain, etc. Sharafat Ali, Fazal Husain and S.B. John sang no more than one or two songs each, but those very songs became the source of their fame. In the earliest days of Pakistan's film industry, Sabiha Khanum, Santosh, Darpan, Nayyar Sultana, and Aslam Pervaiz did excellent work.

The 1960s and 70s were magnificent decades for the film industry in Pakistan. In this period Ahmed Rushdie, Mala, Mehdi Hasan, Masood Rana, Runa Laila, Naheed Akhter, Mehnaz, Tasawwar Khanum, A. Nayyar, and Asad Amanat Ali rose to fame. Waheed Murad became the heart-throb of moviegoers. Rehman, Shameem Ara, Mohammad Ali, Zeba, Shabnam, Nadeem, Shahid, Nushu, and Barbara Sharif delivered memorable performances.

Regional songs such as the songs of fishermen and peasants, wedding songs, *mahia* and *dhola* songs, Sohni Mahniwal, Heer Ranjha, Sassi Pannu and Mirza Sahiban—all these were sung by

Jawad Ahmed, Sanam Marvi, Hania, and Zeb in their villages. Pushto speakers listen happily to Mashooq Sultan, Baloch audiences to Akhter Chanal, and Sindhis to Ma'i Dha'i.

In dance, the senior most practitioner in Pakistan was Madam Azuri, who demonstrated her skill in England and other European countries during British rule in the subcontinent. She continued to teach dance in Pakistan for a few years after Partition. Madam Azuri ended her life in penury and ill health. In Karachi Ghansham sahib taught Bharatnatyam. But the brainiest among them all and the one who continues to teach dance to the new generation to this day, is Sheema Kirmani. Kirmani established a group called Tehrik-e-Nisswan (Women's Movement) which presents dance dramas focusing on women's issues. Eighty-five-year-old Indu Mitha teaches Bharatnatyam. Her daughter Tehrima began to learn dancing from her mother at the age of eight. These days she has her own training unit in the United States. She comes to Pakistan every year and presents new dance items.

Kathak is a dance created in the Moghul era. Maharaj Ghulam Husain used to teach this dance. He had many pupils, boys and girls, but the most prominent among those who gained fame and are still dancing is Naheed Siddiqui. She established a training centre in the UK. For the last 20 years she has been teaching Kathak and other dances to the young in Lahore. Fasihur Rehman is teaching dance in London. Nighat Chaudhry was also a pupil of Maharaj. She too, teaches dance to young people. It is very common for female dance students to stop dancing after they are married. Twenty-year-old Jahanara was a very promising dancer. She died when a burglar shot her in her throat.

The PIA Arts and Dance Academy was founded in the days of Zulfikar Ali Bhutto. It was almost terminated under Zia ul-Haq. Later it was revived, and now it is working again. It has an ensemble of eight boys and eight girls who present all the folk dances of Pakistan accompanied by music, in folk costumes. This ensemble travels to many overseas countries where it stages cultural portraits of Pakistan. It has its own orchestra.

A new form of dance combined with theatre has emerged in Pakistan. It is called Mime. Mimed stories are presented wordlessly in gestures and shadows. This genre has attracted young Pakistanis.

Several NGOs have presented dramas on social issues through the medium of street theatres in urban and rural areas. People stand in a circle with the actors performing in the centre of the circle. Once the play is over, it is time for a question and answer session. Issues highlighted in the performance include family planning and violence against women. The effect of the plays is long-lasting. Madiha Gauhar, Wasim and Rafi Pir Theatre are engaged in presenting this form of theatre.

The history of sculpture goes back at least 7000 years. The 'Dancing Girl', and 'Priest King' are statues found in Mohenjo-Daro. They were created 5000 years ago. The real 'Dancing Girl' is in the National Museum of India at New Delhi where it was sent but was never returned. The two statues are 5000 years old. Inscriptions on pottery, seals, and figurines of this period evidence the fine workmanship of Mohenjo-Daro's craftsmen. Many Pakistani designers are inspired by old inscriptions, whether they are in the Makli or Chokandi necropolis, or the Moghul mosque at Thatta. They use these old motifs in the fabric design they create. The Mehrgarh region of Balochistan has a 7000-year-old history. Excavations in the hills of this area yield fine pottery decorated with patterns, and are almost intact.

Shahid Sajjad was the most highly renowned sculptor in Pakistan. His wooden figures, mother and child among other themes, were carved out with such perfectionism that not a joint was visible in the wood. He had equipped his whole house to serve as a showcase for his sculpture. The sculptor Abbas Shah worked in fibre glass and Rabia Zuberi hewed her sculptures from stone. Amin Gul makes all kinds of statues and jewellery from copper and steel. Abdul Raheem Solangi introduced a new style in sculpture. Qaseem Raheem excelled in micro miniature.

Sculpture now took another aspect. Ceramics were not only decorated with patterns and painted, they were also glazed. Eminent artists like Sheherzad Alam, Talat, and Dabir, even installed furnaces in their homes. In addition to table lamps, new kinds of jars and plates, Dabir even made replicas of famous forts in Pakistan all in ceramics.

Sheherzade Alam was chosen President of the South Asian Ceramic Association. She trained many artists among whom are Amjad Ali Daudpota, Wasima Saleem, Kulsoom Mehmood, Intesar Saleem, Afshan, and Nausheen. Whenever they are asked why they chose this form of the art, the inevitable reply is 'Out of love for the soil of my land.' These artists are going to exhibit their work in Turkey, Scandinavia, Japan, and China. Sheherzade trained first with a teacher in India, and then with another teacher Mohammad Nawaz in Harappa. In addition to the names given so far, Salahuddin of National College has worked extensively with ceramics.

Although Duriya Qazi too has done considerable work in painting and ceramics, she is better known for her work in truck art. All trucks, rickshaws and vans in Pakistan are adorned with paintings. Among the pictures of stylized foliage, owners of these vehicles like to insert portraits of their favourite personalities. For example many Pathan truck drivers have Ayub Khan's portrait at the back of their buses or trucks, as well as a sentimental couplet under it, like: *Teri yaad aai /therey janay kay baad.* Zulfikar Ali Bhutto, Benazir, and many film personalities also come in for similar treatment. Interesting messages commonly seen on the backs of buses etc. are: *Puppoo yar tung na kar, Maa ki dua Jannat ki hawa,* etc. This kind of painting is usually done in South Punjab. Trucks and buses are also decorated with small coloured light bulbs. 'Truck art' as it has come to be known, has gained popularity even worldwide. Small replicas of trucks adorned in this way have eager buyers usually among foreign tourists. Untaught artists of truck art were invited to an exhibition of their work in London where they also gave a demonstration of their art being produced. The show was very popular.

In folk festivals or fairs, puppet shows have gained much

popularity. Two puppeteers sit behind a curtain and pull the strings to make the puppets act. One of the two plays the *dholuk* or drum while the other sings. Both men and women are involved. Pakistani puppeteers were invited for training to China where puppetry has evolved greatly. New stories for the puppet show and new kinds of puppets were created during this training. The Rafi Pir group made puppets the size of human beings. These are seen walking about in folk festivals and fairs, every year. Farooq Qaiser took the art of creating puppets and presenting them in children's theatre to its height. He has been presenting puppet shows on television unfailingly for the last twenty-five years. The main voice in the shows is Farooq Qaiser's own. Masi Musibatai, a female character in the show became famous. The characters Uncle Sargam and Rola also gained a lot of popularity.

Let us now examine the arts and culture of rural Pakistan. After washing their food vessels, women in our villages arrange them on a shelf over the fireplace. The shelf is usually covered with a hand embroidered cloth edged with a crocheted border. Walls are decorated with floral designs in the regional style. Mud stoves are coated with a mixture of water and dung to make them look neat, as though no food was cooked on them. Ovens built by three or four families as a joint endeavour are used by women of the neighbourhood to bake their families' daily bread. Mud is also used to make cooking pots, lamps, pots for holding water and keeping it cool, and tubs for storing wheat. Since most areas of Pakistan now have gas, these mud vessels are used only as ornaments for display. Cow dung cakes are still made in rural areas to be used as fuel and to line and freshen embers in the hookah's cup. These *pathis* or cow dung cakes are made by mixing straw dust with cow dung. Women are so used to making them that all the cow dung cakes turn out round and of the same size. Western tourists take pictures of them and even buy them to take them home. There have been many experiments in making biogas from dung but they were not successful everywhere. Nowadays experiments in making electricity from solar energy are being tried in many places.

Constructing musical instruments is a very delicate craft. In the centre of every town, and not just in Lahore, are made the tabla, *dholak*, *sitar*, *sarinda*, harmonium, *chimta*, *iktara*, and *alghoza*. Folk dances include the Khattak dance of KP, which is a fast and attractive dance accompanied with swords; the Jhoomar comes from southern Punjab; Luddi, Bhangra, and Sammi dances are natives of upper Punjab. In Jhang, men dancing Sammi arrange themselves into the shape of a camel while the dhol and the *kharka* are played. Ho Jamalo is the distinctive dance of Sind. The Dhammal is danced at shrines. The Leva is a popular dance of Balochistan, and the fishermen's dance is its special feature.

Small circuses are usually a part of fairs. They feature mermaids, as well as motorcyclists who perform stunts, riding their motorcycles along vertical 'walls of death'. Small ferris wheels provide inexpensive entertainment to poor children and are found abundantly especially in folk celebrations, fairs, and on the Eids. Despite the progress of time, in the far-flung areas of Pakistan men can be seen even now, going about with a peep show in a wooden box, calling out '*Bara mun ki dhoban dekho, Makkah Medina dekho*' etc.

Let's take a look at regional sports. In rural areas the sports most popular are cock fights, dog fights, donkey cart races, playing cards with or without betting. The rich bet in horse races, go hunting in the forests in groups, for deer, water fowls, partridges, and quail. Wealthy retirees play chess, golf, and bridge. These sports can also be played for stakes.

Now we come to regional children's sports. When I took stock of regional games and their names in all the languages, I realized that although their names changed from language to language, the games themselves remained the same. For example, hide-and seek is known as *chhuppan chhupahee* as well as *aankh macholi*. *Pitthu garam, gulli danda, punj witty, kokla chhupahee, appi dappi, kiri kara*, are all regional names which are different in every regional language, yet they are the same games. Spinning the top is popular among children of every region.

Flying kites is popular all over the country. Nowadays kite strings are glass-coated. Since these are capable of cutting throat, they have been banned. But the ban may be lifted. The bear and snake shows can be found in every town and village. Snake and mongoose fights fascinate both adults and children. Fights between bears and dogs can be blood-curdling, and have been banned by the government.

A common sight in villages is a chair placed under a tree, a mirror attached to the tree trunk, and a barber busy shaving his customer. This spectacle can be seen in towns as well, though less commonly. There are also street dentists who can extract teeth. Professional earwax removers are also available by the wayside. Waiting by the wayside for customers are also masseurs with bottles of oil in their hands. These too are a common sight.

Fawzia Minullah worked at expanding poor children's awareness and enhancing their education through art and colours, in small settlements and in primary schools for the underprivileged. The Japanese government invited Fawzia to Japan on a scholarship and trained her to carry her campaign further.

4

Our Historical Places and Shrines

THE WORD 'LAHORE' CONJURES UP THE IMAGE OF THE SHRINE of Data Gunj Bukhsh. His real name was Abul-Hasan Ali bin Usman al Jalabi al Hajveri al Ghaznavi. It is said that he arrived in Lahore in AH 431, with the purpose of propagating Islam. Travellers to Lahore—no matter which religion they belong to—visit the shrine of Data Sahib to pay their respects. The entrance of the shrine offers a glimpse of the Moghul style of architecture. The door of the shrine, a gift of the Shah of Iran, is decorated with gold and glass. It is said that every month offerings to the shrine add up to an amount of money that could be enough for the total expenditure of Lahore, and the public kitchen of the shrine could feed all of the population of Lahore. Like in other shrines of the country, any individual who spends Rs. 100 to buy a floral cover for the tomb can benefit from this.

On the right bank of the river Ravi is a pavilion, which is in a decrepit state despite the government's efforts to restore it. People who are boating in the river make a stop there. The British used this pavilion as a post office. It is known as Kamran's Pavilion after Kamran Mirza who was the son of Emperor Babar.

Jahangir's tomb can be seen to the right of the Ravi. Jahangir died when he was coming to Lahore from Kashmir in 1627. His wife, Noorjahan, brought his body to the Dilkusha Garden which had been laid out by her. The tomb, built by Shahjahan, is surrounded by acres of garden. Noorjahan's own tomb is close to her husband's. Precious stones embedded in her mausoleum were taken away by Ranjit Singh. Close to Noorjahan's mausoleum is her brother Asif Jah's. Ranjit Singh plucked the gold and semi-precious stones from here too and used it in the pavilion in Hazoori Bagh which he built.

Nobody can see all of Lahore's historical fort in a single visit. This magnificent fort was expanded by four Moghul kings in their time. It houses the Moti Masjid, Naulakha Pavilion, Shah Burj, and Sheesh Mehal. The white marble and sandstone used in it show the influence of Iranian architecture. The glazed tile work, coloured stones, and the dark room where employees lighten the mirror work with lanterns fascinate visitors.

Across from the fort, Aurungzeb Alamgir built the largest mosque of his day. The mosque was constructed at a cost of six hundred thousand rupees. The four minarets of the mosque can be seen from every direction. A look at the wide courtyard paved with red stone lifts the spirit. To the left of the Badshahi Mosque is the mausoleum of Allama Iqbal, much visited by people of all ages who come there to offer *fatiha*. To the right of the mosque is the Shahi Mahalla, a bazaar mostly in a state of disrepair. Close to the Masti Gate is the Maryamzamani Mosque. This was built by Jahangir's mother. Now we proceed to the Chauburji, which is located south of the fort. Its four minarets can be seen from all sides. It was built by Aurungzeb's daughter, Zubaida who used to write poetry under the alias Makhfi.

Past the Kashmiri Bazaar one comes to Masjid Wazir Khan which is being repaired and restored by UNESCO in the same way as Andaroon Lahore and Shahi Hamam are being revitalized by the Agha Khan Funds. The answer to who built Lahore's famous gates is that they too were built by Akbar. The population of common people in Andaroon Sheher, adjacent to the royal fort needed to be guarded too. The Shah Alam Gate which was one of these gates was burned down in the Partition related riots. The Lohari Gate, Shranwala, Musti, Bhaati, and Dehli Gates are safe. The rest are alive only in name. Advancement of industry has turned Andaroon Sheher into small markets and factories. However, the crockery and gold jewellery market remain unaffected so do the shops that make gold and silver leaf. Malik Ayaz had populated the Sowitr Mandi area. Akbar had built Bazaar-e-Hakiman, and Bhaati Gate Maghrabi. Similarly, Raja Jhug Phal helped build gates around Lahore. On Aibak Road is the mausoleum of Qutubuddin Aibak who was the founder of the Delhi Empire, and died when he fell from a horse while playing polo. This mausoleum was in a dilapidated condition; the government of Pakistan has restored it. Five kilometers beyond Mughalpura is the Shalimar Bagh. Shahjahan began its construction in 1637 and completed it in 1641.

There are hundreds of mausoleums in Lahore where the annual *urs* or the death anniversary of the deceased person is commemorated. But Shah Jamal's mausoleum is the only one where the dhol, or drum, is beaten every Thursday and whose Bibi Pak Daman's shrine is also famous.

On the way from Lahore to Shaikhopura, are first the Shaikhopura Fort and then the Hiran Minar garden which was revived thirty years ago. Hiran Minar was built by Jahangir in memory of his favourite deer, Hunss Raj. The Shaikhopura Fort was also Jahangir's creation.

Noorjahan who had ordered the building of Jahangir's mausoleum, had started her own mausoleum as well, but it was not completed in her lifetime. It carries the following couplet:

> *Bur mazar-e-ma ghariban nai chiraghae nai gulae*
> *Nai par-e-parwana sozad nai sada-e-bubulae*

On my mausoleum there is neither lamp nor flowers
Neither the wing of a moth burns, nor is a nightingale heard.

On leaving Lahore behind, Anarkali's white tomb can be seen in the grounds of the Civil Secretariat. It is used as a record room by the government of Punjab.

A little further from Jehlum is a fort which was completed by Sher Shah Suri—the same Sher Shah who built the G.T. Road from Peshawar to Kolkata. 25 kilometres from Chakwal is the Raj Katas Temple, which was the oldest Sanskrit university. After Partition, people built their houses there. When Manmohan

Singh visited Pakistan, the government of Pakistan had some of the area vacated and improved the look of the temple.

We can now proceed to Multan. The Multan Fort is about 2500 years old. On its grounds are the mausoleum of Bahauddin Zakaria, and the mausoleums of Shah Rukn-e-Alam and Shamsuddin Sabzwari. A university is located in the grounds of Shaikh Bahauddin's tomb. It is said that there was a Parmalaat temple in Multan which was thousands year old. Haram Gate is famous like Lahore's red light area.

The oldest temple in Bahawalpur was known as the Krishna Parkash Haveli. An old map of Bahawalpur indicates that what is known as the Bahawalpur Fort was built by Hindu Rajput Ra'ai Jujja Bhatti. Places worth seeing in Bahawalpur are: National Park Uch Shareef, Noor Mehel, Gulzar Mehel, Lal Sohanra Park, and most of all, Fort Darawar. This fort is among the UNESCO protected sites in the world. Its forty arches can be seen from a distance. Fort Darawar was first built by a Hindu Rajput from Jaissalmer, Rai Jujja Bhatti. It came into the possession of the Nawab of Bahawalpur in 1747 and he built a mosque next to it. This mosque was made on the pattern of Moti Masjid in the Red Fort. It is now in ruins.

The Cholistan desert has been watered in places and turned into grasslands. However, huts can be seen spread over large stretches of sandy desert. Every year the Chanan fair is held on seven Thursdays from February to March. The fair is at its peak on the fifth Thursday. Folk artists coming here from different regions consider it an honour to be participating in this fair.

In the Rahim Yar Khan district, there is the Bhong Masjid which received the Aga Khan Award for Architecture for the year 1986, given to it by the Aga Khan Foundation. The history of this mosque shows that it was reconstructed again and again over several generations. Zayed bin Sultan al Nahyan, the ruler of Abu Dhabi built a medical college and hospital in the city of Rahim Yar Khan. The Shaikh Zayed International Airport in Rahim Yar Khan is named after him.

And now we come to Sind. Pakka Qila (fort) of Hyderabad built by Mian Ghulam Shah Kalhoro is politically very famous. Naukot Qila is in the south of Mirpur Khas. It was built by the Talpurs. Qila Kotdiji in Khairpur was built by Sohrab Khan Talpur while Qila Ranikot lies in the district of Jamshoro. It is the largest fort, and was built by Mir Talpur and Mir Murad Ali. Umerkot Fort is famous because the Moghul emperor Akbar was born there. Thatta's Shahjahani Mosque is incomparable for its architectural beauty.

Gwader in Balochistan used to be a part of Oman. Pakistan bought it from Oman in 1958 for $300,000. The fort, Qila Gwader, is located here. The Pannu Fort is in the Ketch district of Balochistan. The Navroz Fort is in Kharan. Qila Abdullah was built by Sardar Abdullah Khan Achakzai. Kalat Fort is still in the possession of the Khan of Kalat. Mir Chakar Fort was built by Sardar Suhbat Khan. The town of Turbat is in the district of Ketch. Members of the Zikri sect go there for their pilgrimage to Koh-e-Murad. Ziarat, a town in Balochistan is where the Quaid-e-Azam spent the last year of his life. The residency in Ziarat, surrounded by juniper trees and the fragrance of lavender, was where the Quaid stayed. In 2013, this historic mansion was set on fire and partially destroyed. Our architects and masons worked hard to restore it to its original stateliness. Every day buses full of tourists and students arrive to see the residency. On its second floor are Quaid-e-Azam's, Miss Fatima Jinnah's and his doctor's bedrooms. On the lower floor are the Quaid's library and the dining and drawing rooms. Qazi Issa, the Baloch leader can be seen with the Quaid in every picture there.

Karachi is an old city, which was once a fishermen's colony. The British built more than two hundred buildings in Karachi, which can still be recognized by their British colonial style. In 2017, this city will be three hundred years old. Karachi's Mohatta Palace was completed in 1927.

Frere Hall has a mural on the ceiling painted by the famous Pakistani artist Sadequain. Karachi was at first Pakistan's only city by the sea, and its beaches were a great attraction for people coming from other parts of the country. Now Gwader and Pasni are also coming up under the guidance of Chinese experts.

After the birth of Pakistan, a national museum and library were founded in Karachi. The city has the Maritime Museum and Auditorium, the Karachi Arts Council, as well as the National Academy of Performing Arts or NAPA, established by Zia Moheyuddin, under Pervez Musharraf. Singers, dancers and actors are trained in this institution. The old name of the building which houses NAPA is the Hindu Gymkhana. Mereweather Tower, the Lighthouse at Manora, NED College (city campus) and the Sind Assembly building were all built under the British Raj.

Now let's have a glimpse of the province Khyber Pakhtunkhwa. As we enter it there is the Attock Fort on the right. Attock is now a part of the Rawalpindi Division. The Moghuls had built this fort on the river as a defence against attackers. The British used to have their cantonment there, and now the Pakistan army has its cantonment in the same place. A separate part of the fort serves as a prison for those the army wishes to incarcerate. Raja Kazim, charged for treason, was imprisoned here. Famous poet Ahmed Faraz who wrote a poem against the army was also locked up here. Moreover, Nawaz Sharif was kept here after Pervez Musharraf overthrew him. The rest of the fort is occupied by the army.

The next site of historical importance is the ruins of Takht Bhai. It is a UNESCO World Heritage Site. On a turning towards Peshawar, there is another fort on the right, which is also under the control of the army. The word Peshawar brings to mind the Qissakhani Bazaar, where houses have carved wooden doors most of which have now been sold off. The original name of the Peshawar fort is the Balahisar Fort. One reason for the historical fame of Sethi House in Peshawar is that political leaders have stayed there. Tajmahal Hotel in Peshawar is famous because Subhash Chandra Bose stayed there for three days before he left for Kabul.

The Shigar, Baltit, and Khaplu forts are in the Gilgit Baltistan region. In addition, there are forts from the eleventh century.

In the mountainous regions of both KP and Gilgit Baltistan, many remains from the Buddhist and Ashoka era can be seen. In Taxila there are the remains of nine Buddhist towns. Ruins of complete grounds of the university and ruins of a residence for mendicants are also extant. The artefacts in the Taxila Museum are worth seeing. In Harappa excavations are being made for the last three decades under the supervision of UNESCO. In the ruins of Mohenjo-Daro, whole foundations of cities, streets and roads, baths, courtyards were carefully excavated to retain their original forms. It is another matter that water from the rice fields of the villages of Larkana is seeping into and damaging the foundations of these remains. The Mohenjo-Daro Museum tells its own distinctive story: the centuries-old bullock cart shown here can be seen rolling along in this area even today.

In the Lahore Museum, the statue of the Fasting Buddha is present in all its uniqueness. In the regions of Hunza and Gilgit, terrorists tried to destroy Buddhist artefacts but they were saved by government efforts. Hinduism along with its temples, gods and goddesses is alive in all the regions where Hindus have a significant population. In the province of Balochistan, two hundred and fifty miles from Karachi, is the Hunglaj Mata Temple, which has been visited by many leaders from India, in addition to the local Hindu population. The Sadhoo Bela Temple in Sukkhar is known worldwide. Similarly, the Shiva and Shri Swami Narayan temples of Karachi are very famous. Since the population of Hindus in Sind is (relatively) high, there are more Hindu temples in this region. Since the population of Tharparkar is two thirds Hindu, temple bells and *bhajans* or hymns can be heard every evening. Not a single Jain temple has survived in Lahore. The last temple was destroyed in the 1992 riots. The small Jain population of Lahore confines itself to offering everyday prayers as well as those on religious occasions in their homes. Although there are none in Lahore, there do exist a few small temples in the villages of Gujranwalla and Gujrat, however, inside people's houses.

The famous Sikh holy place, Panja Sahib, is in Hasanabdal. There are six gurdwaras in Nankana Sahib. Kartarpura gurdwara is in the Narowal district, Kujbhati and Patshahi gurdwaras are in Karachi, Chota Mufti Baqar is in Lahore, and there are more gurdwaras in village Bhawan Patashi. On religious occasions Sikhs from all over the world come to pray here. They stay, cook, sleep, as well as pray in the gurdwaras. The tomb or *samadhi* of Ranjit Singh in Lahore is also an outstanding edifice.

All areas in Pakistan have both Sunni and Shia mosques. Many mosques have been built by Pakistani workers abroad who thereby invest in their afterlife. Similarly, *imambargahs* exist in every village, and here and there are *eidgahs* as well. Now a mention must be made of the most important places. In Lahore's Iqbal Park is the Minar-e-Pakistan which was built in the very same spot where the Lahore Resolution (now called the Pakistan Resolution) was first passed in 1940. Mukhtar Masood was a member of the Building Committee. The second important place is Quaid-e-Azam's mausoleum in Karachi. Within this complex are the tombs of Fatima Jinnah, Noorul-Amin, Liaquat Ali Khan, Begum Rana Liaquat Ali Khan, and Sardar Abdul Rab Nishtar. The third of these important places or edifices is the Faisal Mosque which has come to symbolize Islamabad.

The minarets of this mosque can be seen from every part of the city. The mosque was built with funds gifted to Pakistan by the late Shah Faisal of Saudi Arabia. It was designed by a Turkish architect but the inscriptions are the work of Pakistani artists Sadequain and Guljee. Islamabad is a valley in the Margala Hills where the federal government's central offices are located. Also sited in Islamabad are the National Art Gallery, Lok Virsa History Museum, and an auditorium gifted by the Chinese Government. There are also six universities and hundreds of colleges and schools in this capital city. The whole city, up to the airport, can be viewed from Daman-e-Koh and the Monal Restaurant. Slums at one corner or another of every sector in Islamabad tell the tale of Afghan refugees who have built and are living in mud houses in practically all the cities of Pakistan.

Now let us mention places of tourists' interest in Pakistan. About fifty kilometres from Islamabad is the picturesque city of Murree, visited by tourists from all over Pakistan, especially in summer. Mall Road in Murree resembles Mall Road in Shimla. Patriata is situated a little higher than Murree. If one travels in the direction of Abbottabad, one finds trees that seem to cover even the upper reaches of the tall mountains which guard Nathiagali, offering their salutations to the traveller. This situation continues until Kala Bagh. A little further is the city of Abbottabad where there is an Army Cantonment as well as a medical college and hospital. Beyond Abbottabad and at a higher elevation is Thandyani which sometimes receives snowfall in winter. After passing Malakand one arrives in Swat which is known as Pakistan's Switzerland. Vestiges of a Buddhist era can be found frequently in Swat and Mingora. Relics of Ashoka's reign are present. There used to be waterfalls and apple trees at every few paces. These still exist, but the landscape here and in Malam Jabba, which is the highest region of Swat, has been marred by terrorists.

In winter there is snowfall in Malam Jabba. Pakistanis and foreigners come here for skating. The trout fish is farmed in Kaghan and Naran. In the Kaghan Naran valley, glaciers often melt in summer. They even slide down and fall, blocking roads. Military helicopters are then deployed to move people to Mansehra.

From Mansehra one can go to Besham, and as one climbs higher, one arrives in Gilgit where one can enjoy the taste of fresh, luscious apricots. In the Gilgit and Hunza area the Aga Khan Foundation has done a great deal of work in the education and health areas. It has given special attention to girls' education. All this has been done under the leadership of Shoaib Sultan.

Further up is Deosai. It has a national park, and is the highest plateau in the world after Tibet. It is a beautiful place where rare fauna and flora can be found. There used to be a monarchy in Hunza, which was terminated during the rule of Zulfikar Ali Bhutto. Old palaces in Hunza and Skardu have been furnished with modern amenities to accommodate tourists. Shangrila Hotel has been there for 30 years. The presence of hotels has boosted tourism a good deal. The Satpara Lake of Skardu and the Upper Kachura Lake beyond Shangrila present a refreshing scenery.

We cannot leave Kaghan and Naran without visiting Lake Saif-ul-Malook. It is more beautiful than any Swiss lake. Thirty years back the mountainous path to this lake could only be negotiated either on horseback or on foot. But now one can take a jeep to get to the Lake. Hidden among the rocks in Kaghan is the Ansoo Jheel (Tear Lake) which is shaped like a tear. Rush Lake in Gilgit Baltistan is the world's highest alpine lake. The Hanna Lake of Balochistan is close to the city of Quetta. The beautiful Zulzul Lake of Azad Kashmir was created when a mountain was brought down by the earthquake, burying 1200 people under it.

The Munchar Lake, the largest freshwater lake not only in Sind but in all of Pakistan, is in the district of Dadu. It has not received the care that it deserves, yet migratory birds arrive here in large numbers. The Haleji Lake in the district of Thatta, close to Karachi was originally supplied with freshwater (it was a saline lake) to provide water to Karachi. It is visited by a very large number of waterfowls.

The salt mine at Khewra which lies in the Salt Range, is the second largest salt mine in the world. Tourists and students come from all over Pakistan to visit this mine in which a mosque and a restaurant are built of salt. The hills in which the mines are located are a rich reservoir of fossils. Fort Munro is a hill station in Dera Ghazi Khan. It is situated at a height of 6,470 feet above sea level.

Pakistan has numerous shrines, but the shrines of Sufi poets occupy a special place in history. One of these houses the tomb of Shah Latif. It is full of devotees all the year round. Shah Latif was born in 1689 and was an adherent of Hafiz. His poetry has been translated into countless languages all over the world.

Sachal Sarmast was born in 1739. He wrote Sufi poetry in seven languages. His mausoleum is in the village Daraza, located in Khairpur district and has been populated by his devotees since it was built. Among modern poets, Shaikh Ayaz is a revolutionary poet and is known all over the world.

In Khyber Pakhtunkhwa the names of Khushhal Khan Khattak and Rehman Baba are famous on account of their revolutionary poetry. Their mausoleums were attacked by terrorists but the government soon had them repaired with the assistance of the poets' followers. The Charsadda University and a library have been named after Khushhal Khan Khattak. Among modern Pakhtoon poets Amir Hamza Shunwari, Ghani Khan, and Ajmal Khatak are also well known for their revolutionary poetry. Historically, the Pathans of the Frontier always warred with the British. The same mood prevails in their poetry.

In Balochistan, the work of Sufi poet Mast Tawakkali has the status of a classic. He wrote poetry in both Balochi and Saraiki. He is widely believed to have been passionately in love with Sammo. Mast's poetry resonates in the desert areas of Balochistan in the songs of the desert dwellers. Mast Tawakkali was born in Mand, a far flung village of the tribal area. He was Balochistan's first poet whose poetry of love was on the lips of the common man living among the mountains.

Next, came the revolutionary poet Gul Khan Naseer, and then

the blend of the romantic and revolutionary Ata Shad, an unrivalled poet of Balochi and Urdu. In Punjab, Baba Bulleh Shah was born in Uch in the year 1680. His mausoleum is in Qasur. His poetry with its tone of rebellion tore away the veil of hypocrisy from the faces of the self-proclaimed religious leaders of the time. Punjab produced many Sufi poets. Baba Fareed was born in 1179. Baba Guru Nanak, the founder of the Sikh religion, is also acclaimed as a Sufi. He was born in 1469. Waris Shah, who is famous for his *Heer*, was born in 1722. Later poets wrote *Heer* in their own style but none could rival Waris Shah. The tomb of Waris Shah's Heer is in Jhang. Waris Shah himself is buried in Jandiala Sher Khan near Sheikhupura. Mian Mohammad Buksh wrote *Saiful Mulook*. The exceptionality of all these poets lies in that their poetry is still read in its original rhythm. Baba Ghulam Fareed's mausoleum is in Pakpatan. It is said that when on the day of the *Urs* the door opens at midnight, the first hundred visitors who enter the tomb will go straight to heaven. Many eager devotees, wishing to be among the first hundred jump from the roof to get there, and break their legs in the attempt. Khwaja Ghulam Fareed's tomb is in Mithankot.

All over Pakistan, even in villages, people know the verses of Sufi poets by heart. Singers such as Abida Perveen, Allan Faqir, Mohammad Yusuf, Hamid Ali Bela, Akhtar Chanal, and Mashooq Sultan, have rendered this poetry in song, popularizing it not just in Pakistan but also in other countries. Foremost among these singers was Nusrat Fateh Ali Khan who received some of the highest awards for his performances.

There are too many shrines in Pakistan for each to be detailed.

At every few paces a pennant can be seen over a tomb which keeps expanding gradually. The number of devotees also grows, and so does the number of handkerchiefs tied to branches of nearby trees. At some point an *urs* is introduced into this evolving lore.

5

Our Theatre, Film and Modern Innovations

IN STAGE DRAMAS LIKE SHAKUNTALA AND INDAR SABHA, THERE was always song and dance, which people called live song and dance. Courtesy and refinement were a given in the culture of Lucknow. After the establishment of Pakistan there was chaos on the cultural scene. In those days the 'radio drama' became so popular that on Saturday nights shopkeepers would close their business for the day early at 8.30 p.m., in order to rush home where they could listen to the play being broadcasted on the radio. Those were days when there were no transistors; just one radio was there in every household. *Akhyan* was a drama written in Punjabi and broadcasted on the radio. It became so popular that numerous requests were received for repeating the broadcast. It was written by Rafi Peer who presented it on the Art Council's small stage. Its popularity was heightened by the fact that Rafi Peer himself played the leading role in both the stage and broadcasted versions.

Imtiaz Ali Taj was the head of the Arts Council. He wrote the famous play *Anar Kali*, which was also staged. Concurrently, Khwaja Moinuddin was writing his own dramas in Karachi. The first of these was *Lal Qilae say Lalu Khet tak*. It portrayed the contrasts and mutual relationships between Sindhi, Punjabi, Pashtu, and Urdu speaking people in a most entertaining way. His play *Mirza Ghalib Bunder Road par*, which took a humorous overview of two centuries, was no less witty and engaging. His third play commissioned by Agha Nasir in the days of Ayub Khan was *Taleem-e-Balghan* (Adult Education). This play has so far been presented about twenty times on stage and television.

While Faiz Ahmed Faiz was the head of the Lahore Arts Council, Safder Mir, Farrukh Nigar Aziz, and Kamal Ahmed Rizvi used to write plays and acted in them on stage. Ashfaq Ahmed, Bano Qudsia, Anwar Sajjad, and Intezar Husain also wrote plays. This was the age when serious plays were written and appreciated. The politics of Pakistan greatly influenced the country's literature, art, and theatre. In 1973, when Zulfikar Ali Bhutto was in power and the Constitution of Pakistan had been passed, Munnoo Bhai wrote the drama *Juloos*, which was staged but did not gain popularity. About this time Bhutto was making agreements with Middle Eastern countries to send Pakistani labourers and other workmen there. Subsequently, people who were poor workmen in Pakistan were able to send home large quantities of funds from the Middle Eastern countries they had found work in. The result was that many Pakistani families who had previously been homeless were able to build villas for themselves. With this as the theme Yunus Jawaid wrote the play *Dubai Chalo*. It became such a hit that its film version ran for one hundred weeks.

In the prevailing atmosphere writers of humorous stage plays had a field day. Cinemas went out of business. Shopkeepers and other fans were so taken with Ali Aijaz and Nanha's performance that they were willing to spend Rs. 500 on a ticket for a show. About the same time a parallel theatre was created by Aslam Azhar, Madiha Gauher, and Sheema Kirmani. Under Zia ul-Haq, showing these dramas could lead to arrest and imprisonment. So they had to be performed covertly. Despite the restrictions, the Ajoka theatre group produced dramas on themes like violence against women and other such scourges of society. Educated individuals took to this genre of theatre and saw no others.

The popularity of cinema was plummeting, while theatre prospered. But it was rowdy, slapstick comedy that flourished in these theatres. The government tried to control it but it was too late. Boisterous entertainment was catching on in other cities too. Humorous stage solos came into vogue and Mueen Akhter presented some good stage shows in this genre. He passed away in 2011. Umer Sharif's drama *Bakra qiston par* was popular in both Pakistan and India. Anwar Maqsood and Bushra Ansari presented their solo stage shows in the Middle East as well. On the one hand the Punjabi Thumka drew large audiences, and on the other, Anwar Maqsood's humorous dramas were blockbusters.

In 1964, Pakistan television initiated its programmes with three hours of viewing, six days a week (no transmissions on Saturdays). All these programmes were live, and for the first time the Pakistani public was supplied entertainment they could turn on at home. During the 1965 war between India and Pakistan, Noorjahan's military songs became very popular.

This was the period when Ashfaq Ahmed, Bano Qudsia, Anwar Sajjad, Haseena Mueen, Fatima Suraiya Bajia, and Hameed Kashmiri's dramas, and the prose writings of Munto, Ghulam Abbas, Ahmed Nadeem Qasmi, and Altaf Fatima, presented in dramatic form, became very popular. The most popular serial was Shaukat Siddiqui's novel *Khuda ki Basti* with the theme of resettlement of refugees in Pakistan from India.

Among humorous television productions Kamal Ahmed Rizvi's *Alif Noon*, Anwar Maqsood's many stage shows and serials with Mueen Akhter and Bushra Ansari were extremely popular. Saleem Nasir's acting in *Angan Terha* was much lauded. Nasir died in 1989. Haseena Moeen gave Pakistan Television memorable serials like *Shehzori*, *Uncle Urfi*, *Zer Zabar Pesh*, *Unkahi*, *Tanhaiyan*, *Dhoop Kinarae*, *Aahut*, and *Kasak*. Fatima Suraiya Bajya focused on wedding rituals in her dramas. Notable among her dramas are *Shama*, *Afshan*, and *Aroosa*. Bajya died on 10 February 2016.

The series of TV dramas which was presented by Mohammad Nisar Husain and broadcasted every Saturday for many years became classic. They were followed by the serials. Amjad Islam Amjad's *Waris* and Asghar Nadeem Saiyid's *Chand Grihan* acquired fame beyond the country's borders. Abdul Qadir Junejo and Noorul Huda Shah wrote beautiful dramas on the themes of Sindhi traditions and rituals and violence against women. Of these, *Jungle*, *Deevaren*, and *Marvi* gained much popularity. Athar Shah Khan and Ataul Haq Qasmi's humorous serials were successful. *Intezar Farmaiyae*, *Hello Hello*, *Kuchwa aur Khargosh* were some of Athar Shah Kahan Jedi's plays that became famous.

In the year 2002, the government of Pakistan allowed private TV channels to transmit their own content. Indus Vision was the first private satellite channel to start transmissions in Pakistan. Others followed suit. Some newspapers started their own channels, and competed with each other. Political themes were important for them, but because every TV company could operate four channels, dramas and interviews (usually of political personalities) were transmitted. However, PTV would sometimes broadcast literary and musical programmes.

PTV transmitted children's programmes and operated a cartoon channel as well. It also presented a good deal of material on history and the Pakistan Movement. *Taabir, Akhri Chatan, Shaheen,* were good historical serials in which many actors gave excellent performances. The number of religious channels increased. Saleem Ahmed also wrote a serial on a religious and historical theme.

Several filmmakers had migrated from Bombay (Mumbai) to Lahore at the time of Partition. Shaukat Husain Rizvi established Shahnoor Studios in Lahore. *Phaeray* was Pakistan's first Punjabi movie. Noorjahan made *Dopatta* and *Chunway*. Masood Pervaiz, Khwaja Khursheed Anwar, Qateel Shifaee, and Ahmed Rahi played important roles in making films. In most of these films the central role was played by Noorjahan. Later she stopped acting but continued to record songs until a few years before her death. Among her children, her daughter, Zille Huma, opted for singing as her career.

Pakistan's first colour film was *Naila*. The movie *Arman*

celebrated its platinum jubilee (was shown for 75 weeks). *Arman* took actor Waheed Murad to the heights of popularity and fame. Pervaiz Malik, the director, made several films after *Arman* among which were *Intekhab*, *Pehchan*, *Talash*, and *Anmol*. He was the only film director to be awarded the Pride of Performance by the Pakistan government.

Pakistani films in those days showed club dances, and seaside scenes in which actresses appeared in swimming costumes. The year 1977 brought hardship to Pakistani movies. Zia ul-Haq's government imposed restrictions on literature, television, as well as film. The curbs were so rigorous that filmmakers finally turned to making humorous Punjabi movies. At first good Punjabi films were produced, such as *Sher Khan*, *Chun Waryam*, *Kalia*, and *Dhee Rani*. *Maula Jat* ran for a year.

The following can be included among names of prominent directors in Pakistan's film industry: Jan Mohammad, Jawaid Fazil, Shabab Keranvi, Nazarul Islam, S.M.Yusuf, Hasan Tariq, Iqbal Yusuf, Khalil Qaiser, S. Sulaiman, Riaz Shahid, and Khurshid Anwar.

Producer Saiyid Noor tried to sustain the enervated film industry of Pakistan, the scene of whose collapse was reflected in deserted cinemas which were being replaced by new plazas. People yearned for Hasan Tariq, Habib Jalib, Riaz Shahid, Mohammad Ali, Zeba, Rani, Shabnam, Nadeem, and Waheed Murad. Meanwhile they watched all kinds of movies on cable television.

Then came the age of short films. Young directors made and exhibited short movies. Film festivals were arranged. Shoaib Mansoor's *Khuda kae liyae* and *Bol* provided encouragement to other young filmmakers. More short films like *Zinda Bhag*, *Dukhtar*, and *Namaloom Afraad* were made. People's tastes changed. Fortune smiled on the deserted cinemas. The film *Manto* made some kind of a world record. *Dukhtar* merited international awards. In 1958 Faiz Ahmed Faiz and A.J. Kardar had made the film *Jago Hua Savera*, which to this day is regarded as a classic. In the 1960s Sindhi movies were also made. But then this particular light died out. Pashtu movies were popular not only in Pakistan but also in the Middle East; their market was the large number of Pathan labourers who worked in the Middle Eastern countries. Later, the number of Pushto films declined, for cinemas were being torched. However, Pushto films revived in 2016.

However, the dying light of the local film has now begun to rekindle. According to one survey, 50 Pushto films were made in the last 70 years. The number of Sindhi films made in this period is 26; of Urdu films 643, and of Punjabi films 709.

Sharmeen Ubaid took the lead in making ground-breaking documentaries. Her first documentary was about throwing acid on a woman, a well-known way of punishing a woman in the subcontinent. The second was about honour-killing. Both these films won the Oscar and earned fame all over the world. Mehreen Jabbar became known for her *Ramchand Pakistani*. Sabiha Sumar made a film on the theme of Partition. Actors from both India and Pakistan took part in it. Ubaidullah Baig made many films on Pakistan's culture, and tourism. 38 of DFP's (Directorate of Films and Publications) films won international awards.

The computer was introduced in Pakistan some 25 years ago. It was followed by the Internet. Subsequently, the mobile phone arrived in all its variety. The IPhone appeared, then came useful sites like the Facebook, Twitter, and Skype. Computers appeared that could take dictation; they came with software that could detect and correct spelling mistakes and software that could expose plagiarism. Games like chess and bridge could be played on the computer. Even though gambling is illegal in Pakistan, there is no law against online gambling; and so numerous Pakistanis gamble on the computer.

Despite the proscription, gambling is a favoured pastime in Pakistan. The rich bet on racehorses, play tambola in their clubs, hotels, or even on mobile phones. The very poor even sit on roads and learn about betting and making their fortune from diviners and fortune tellers. Officially all kinds of betting is forbidden. All the same countless people, old or young, in urban or rural areas, can be seen gambling. There is an official raffle for 'prize bonds' every third month. The lucky winner can collect sums of money as high as fifty or a hundred thousand. Afraid of being robbed, the not so well off winner is often known to sell his winning prize bond for a few thousand rupees, rather than risk travelling to collect his prize. Commercial companies and TV channels hold programmes in which lavish prizes such as a car or a house are given. There is no check on these, and everybody prospers and is happy. There are lotteries the world over, but they are prohibited in Pakistan. The YouTube too was banned until recently.

Cartoons in advertisements used to be popular in the past. Now cartoon films are made and released universally. In Pakistan, Sharmeen Ubaid has made the country's first animated feature film, *Teen Bahadur*. Now cartoon figures are introduced even in regular, non-cartoon movies. Walt Disney's cartoon films are still popular the children, and so are the Harry Potter movies.

Japan was the first to make Judo and Karate movies. Soon they became popular in the subcontinent as well. Some films and television dramas based on science fiction are being made in Pakistan but their number is small. Jamal Shah is making a movie on the political and social situation in Swat. Farjad Nabi is another name that is linked to individual endeavours in filmmaking.

6

Our Cuisine

IN THE OLDEN DAYS IT WAS CUSTOMARY TO EAT ROTI LEFT OVER the night before, with some leftover curry. This practice was common to people in all the provinces of Pakistan. In Sind and Punjab leftover or fresh roti could be eaten with some *lassi* or yogurt drink as well. Homes which possessed buffaloes would send *lassi* to neighbouring houses where there were no buffaloes or milch cows. In those days it was common practice to bury dung cakes or firewood in hot ashes. The next morning the fire was fanned through a bellows, or little children were sent off with a ladle to a neighbour's house to fetch a piece of live coal. In urban areas where there were no dairy cattle, people had their roti with tea. In some households leftover roti spread with ghee and water was heated and eaten in place of paratha. Leftover pieces of roti were never wasted. They were collected in a bag and when there were enough of them they were placed on the fire with some water. Spices were added and the concoction was cooked like *haleem*, or boiled with milk and sugar to be turned into a sort of kheer that children like.

In the villages women are up before dawn. Farmers usually breakfast on roti and pickles before leaving for the fields. Women workers in the fields dig up potatoes, pluck peas, okra, and zucchini; plant rice seedlings; pluck cotton buds; pluck *motia* jasmine flowers in the summer; and gather round red chilies. Those who come early to the fields with their men bring with them freshly made roti, pickles, and *lassi* or yogurt drink. Women who are busy working with or without their men, making carpets on the loom, embellishing the *khussa* shoe with embroidery, or doing other fancy embroidery like shadow work etc., or working with men to make door screens or blinds, prepare roti and leave it in reed baskets. When the children come home from school, they eat the roti with sugar or with pickles. Vegetables and lentils are eaten as daily fare in the region stretching from Nagarparker to Gilgit. However, a goat, a sheep or chicken is slaughtered when guests are expected.

In many cities, office goers take their lunch with them in lunch boxes. Labourers who work far away from their homes lunch on hot paratha and tea at a roadside eatery. At the end of the day when they finish their work they might take a bath at a public bath, eat *naan* and boiled gram or gram lentils at a roadside eatery. In the winter many labourers eat jalebis soaked in milk at the local eatery. Along the routes taken by truck drivers are special eateries where goat meat is cooked in ghee. The truck drivers' favourite drink after their meal is tea brewed with milk and sugar. Pathans, no matter where they hail from, are particularly fond of mutton. They enjoy meat with plenty of fat and after this, they have black tea.

From Sukkhar to Gwader in the province of Sind the Palla fish as well as all the vegetables of the season are eaten. In Sind, the guar bean is eaten all through summer. Mustard plant leaves (*sarsoon saag*), is now consumed all over the country though formerly it used to be eaten mainly in Punjab, along with *cholaee saag* and roti made of corn flour. In Karachi pomfret is the preferred sea food of the rich. Bitter gourd cooked with minced meat or lots of onions is a summer specialty.

Whether it is Lahore, Peshawar, Quetta, or Hyderabad, pulao in all its different forms is much relished. The Sindhi biryani has in it dried plums, potatoes, and equal amounts of rice and meat. The poor who cannot afford meat very often, cook broken rice, sometimes with gram and sometimes with potatoes. They eat this with *raita*. Formerly chicken curry and biryani used to be the favorite at wedding functions and other large parties. However, nowadays *tikkas*, barbecued *seekh kebabs*, fried fish with oiled *naans* are more the norm.

At parties held in homes, food items include *karhi* and rice, *koftas*, vegetable pulao, *haleem*, *dahi phulki* or *dahi barra*, *nihari*, *pa'ai*, *kunna*, mincemeat with bitter gourd or capsicums, tomato *kut*. Many households also prepare Chinese cuisine. Chinese restaurants can be found in every city of Pakistan.

Previously it was the custom for families to eat sitting on the floor with the food laid on a *dastarkhan* or sheet of cloth meant for the purpose. But the dining table and chairs soon replaced the *dastarkhan* in households that could afford them. Nowadays, in a growing number of families both men and women go out to work. So families usually eat together only on holidays. In many households in the rural areas the husband is served his food as he reclines on his bed, even now. The sons eat next, and last of all, the wife and daughters have their meal sitting on low stools in the kitchen. In Pathan households the men are sent their food in the men's quarter. It is the servant's job to change the water in the hookah, barbeque *tikka* and kebabs for the master and bring them to him, press his legs, and massage his body. The women in the household usually eat vegetables and lentils. Served frequently in the tribal chief's guest house or sitting room is a roasted goat stuffed with chicken, rice, quail and partridge. From Balochistan to Gilgit and Khyber Pakhtunkhwa, truck drivers to tribal chiefs are in the habit of stuffing their cheeks with snuff which they keep sucking. Marijuana is also consumed in Punjab mostly in its rural areas. In the summer season bhang is consumed mixed with *char maghz* and milk. People in urban places drink cool beverages made with tamarind, plum, or *tukhm balanga* (sweet basil seeds) in the evening.

The customary breakfast today is different from what it was in the past. Many middle class people have parathas with yogurt or leftover curry from the night before. More affluent or educated people have bread and butter, egg, and cereal. *Halwa puri*, usually made at eateries or by vendors is a favourite holiday breakfast. Barley, or wheat bread when available, with garlic and red chilly chutney or pickles is commonly eaten for breakfast in Tharparkar. Guests are served bread spread with ghee, with garlic and red chilly chutney (relish) and goat's milk. Meat is not eaten in Hindu households, so they confine themselves to vegetables.

Rice bread is a favourite in Sind, Chitral, and Kalash households. They make their roti the way pancakes are made. The Kalash women wear many bead necklaces. They make these necklaces and their distinctive caps themselves. The Kalash are known to this day for their unique culture. They have their own festivals, rituals, and ceremonies.

The rich, the government officials, and landlords are fond of hunting. They bring home deer, wild duck, partridge, and quail from the hunt which their servants roast and serve. They share all this exotic food with their distinguished guest. The peasants who help in the hunt go home to eat their dry bread. Sometimes the sons of the rich hand them their leftovers.

In the past there used to be hand-driven flour mills in homes. The women of the house used to grind their grain on these to make flour for bread. However, now flour is available in every market and every city.

Many areas have their own specialties in food. For example, Kashmir is known for its *roghan josh*, *gosht gushtaba*, and *shab daig*. There are some seven varieties of *saag*. These are cooked with garlic and ghee in all of Khyber Pakhtunkhwa. Kashmir's *kulchai*, *roghani naan*, *baqar khani*, *naan* with mincemeat or vegetables, are now available all over Pakistan. Vendors in every city sell Kashmiri chai. Saffron, where obtainable, is used to make *zarda* which is served at wedding parties. Like Ziarat, many herbs can be found in Kashmir. Foreign tourists pluck these to take home with them. Since alcohol is prohibited, Muslims obtain it through permits for non-Muslims, even buying it at twice the price. In many wealthy households numerous drinks are available. In the days of Zia ul-Haq, many writers and poets were arrested for smelling of alcohol. They were quickly and quietly released when a rich or important man interceded on their behalf. Even opium was not available in the early days of Zia ul-Haq's government. Now it can be obtained even from *hakeems* and grocers. In the villages experiments in making alcoholic drinks in *matkas* or earthen pots are frequently made. They are not always successful, and one reads in the newspapers, '40 people died on drinking homemade liquor'. However, village specialists can sometimes produce good liquor. This is made with jaggery, grapes and apples.

On religious occasions, children are sent for from madrasas. They are fed gram and rice pulao. The Indian *thali* is gaining popularity here. It is a plate on which vegetables, lentils, rice, and pickles are served. Beef or mutton trotters *(pa'ai), harissa, nihari,* and *haleem* are eaten mainly in winter. They are accompanied with *suji ka halwa, daal halwa,* potato sweet potato or pumpkin kheer. Date and walnut halwas are also made in the winter, so is *muzaffar* made with vermicelli. Rice with jaggery and kheer made with sugarcane juice are also very popular. Many poor people eat slices of *garma* with their *naan*. The rich are partial to mutton and goat meat.

7

Our Festivals

THE MUCH AWAITED AND MOST POPULAR FESTIVAL IN THE Muslim world is Eid-ul-Fitar. Muslims fast reverentially for the whole month of Ramzan, and say the nightly *taravih* prayers. At the pre-dawn meal known as *sehri* they spend time with their families preparing for the fast that starts with dawn. Even those Muslims who are not regular with their five daily prayers, say them regularly during Ramzan. Preparations for *iftar*, the sundown fast-breaking meal, start with the afternoon in the market and in households. Numerous households send out trays full of *iftari* to mosques where the poor come to break their fast. Many people from the older generation break their fast and say their prayers with these people rather than in their own homes. Formerly women used to say their *taravih* prayers at home, but now separate arrangements for women are made in city mosques so that they too can say them there. The end of the nightly recitation of the Quran at *taravih* prayers is celebrated on or around the 27th of Ramzan. In their homes, children and adults read the whole Quran—from beginning to end—at least once during this holy month. The bulk of *zakat*, the obligatory contribution for the deserving poor, and *khairat* the optional charity, is given during Ramzan. In the opulent households of the cities *iftari* is prepared and served to large numbers of the

71

common people. For the rich not only are *iftar* parties held at home and in restaurants, now even pre-dawn *sehri* parties have become common. But such activities are confined to the rich.

Before Zia ul-Haq took the reins of government, railway stations and small restaurants used to arrange a curtained space within their precincts for food to be served to those who were not fasting. After the proscription on publicly serving food in Ramzan, hospitals did provide food to their patients, but for caregivers who came with the patients to look after them there was no place where they could obtain or eat food. However, nowadays the many well-wishers who provide *iftari* for hundreds of people also leave behind something for the caregivers.

During Ramzan only bakeries remain open. General stores retail different kinds of pre-cooked parathas that only need to be heated. Food is cooked only in households where there are children. In the rest the stove is not lighted except at *sehri* and *iftar*. In Ramzan sweetmeat shops expand to include space beyond their precincts, where they start selling samosas, *kachori*, *pakoras, jalebis, phaini*, chicken and vegetable rolls, pizzas, and sandwiches in the afternoon, well ahead of *iftar* time at sundown. People buy these and either break their fast at the shop itself or carry them home to be eaten there. In ordinary households, people break their fast with a date or a pinch of salt at *iftar*, and have their dinner after they have said their *maghrib* or sundown prayers. At *sehri* it is usual for them to eat parathas with the night's leftover curry, yogurt, and tea. *Dahi bara* is a favourite addition to this fare. If Ramzan falls in summer, cold drinks including drinks made of tamarind, plums, almonds, fresh lime, and many others are much relished. They are sold in marketplaces and also prepared at home.

Thirty or forty years ago vermicelli for Eid was made at home. Nowadays it is made commercially and sold at the grocery or the supermarket. When the Eid moon is sighted, the night before Eid, children are taken out for special shopping. Women buy bangles, and have henna applied to their hands either at beauty parlours or at stalls in the bazaars set up by young boys and girls. Often women of a family get together and the application of henna becomes joyous occasion in somebody's house. *Sheer khorma* is a special Eid dish, like the Christmas cake. Housewives cut up dried fruit and soak dates in milk the night before Eid, to make *sheer khorma* early morning on Eid. Other food items like *chana chaat*, kebabs, *dahi bara*, etc. are prepared for guests.

Young boys and adults bathe, change into new clothes, and perfumed with *ittar,* head for the mosque to say their Eid prayers. The Sunnah decrees that those on their way to the mosque should follow a different route to return, thus finding and giving alms to as many poor beggars as possible. A certain amount of money, specified a week previously by the Ulema Council, and known as *fitra*, has to be given as alms by the worshippers before the start of the Eid prayers. After the prayers it is customary to visit the graveyard before returning home. At the graveyard people lay flowers on the graves of their loved ones and others, and pray by the graves.

Formerly, scanning the sky for the Eid moon used to be a

common ritual. Men, women and children would climb to the roofs of their houses and look for the slim, faint crescent that heralds the first day in the month of Shawwal, which is Eid-ul-Fitar. On sighting the moon people prayed and embraced each other.

However, now customs have changed. Few go up to their roofs to look for the new moon anymore. Instead people sit in front of the TV set and wait for the official announcement that proclaims the sighting of the moon. Once the day is announced people phone, and now even skype their friends and relatives living locally or in distant parts of the world to felicitate them.

Children are given *eidi*, or small sums of money by their parents, after Eid prayers. After this happy ritual people visit their relatives, especially the elderly ones, their friends, and neighbours. It is customary to embrace each other on Eid when they meet.

Almost inevitably, there is disagreement among the Ulema on the sighting of the moon. Consequently it is rare for the whole country of Pakistan to celebrate Eid on the same day. In places like northern Waziristan, Fata, and Kohistan, Ramzan starts a day earlier, so Eid too comes earlier than elsewhere in Pakistan. Usually these people follow the practice in Saudi Arabia. On every festival, and especially on Eid, daughters or sons-in-law are sent Eid clothes, sweetmeats, bangles, and vermicelli. This is also called *Eidi*.

Eid-ul-Azha has an ambience totally different from that of

Eid-ul-Fitar. Families prepare to welcome relatives who are returning from the Haj pilgrimage. From the first of Zil Haj to the tenth, children are happily involved in accompanying their parents when they go to buy their sacrificial animals, adorning, feeding and taking them for walks around their neighbourhood. At night they demand to hear the story of Hazrat Ibrahim's sacrifice from their parents again and again. The Eid-ul-Azha sacrifice is a religious duty for all Muslims who can afford it. Many who can afford the expense perform the sacrifice for their deceased parents as well, in order to give them a better after-life. However, prices have been rising, and the number of goats has gone down. Now people buy portions in a cow—which becomes a group sacrifice. Some people say that animal sacrifice, is incumbent only on those who are performing the Haj. For the rest it is a Sunnah and optional. Instead of carrying out the sacrifice, many affluent people donate an amount of money equal to the price of the animal to the Edhi Centre or spend it on buying fans for a mosque. Following the Saudi Arabian tradition some people sacrifice a camel. The Sunnah requires that one third of the sacrificed animal's meat be given to the poor, one-third to relatives, and one-third kept back for one's own household. However, the trend is to send parts of the animal from one house to another to flaunt one's own prosperity. Many households keep the meatiest parts for themselves. Some people fill up their freezers with enough meat to last them for months, forgetting that the spirit behind the sacrifice demands that it should benefit mainly the poor.

We have a strange custom that people go for Haj and Umrah pilgrimages even when their age has made it difficult for them to walk. To educate the Haj pilgrims, the Ministry of Religious Affairs organizes a training course, and with it the ministry arranges for all kinds of injections and medication as well. Every group of pilgrims is led by a *muallim*, approved by the Ministry. Haj and Umra pilgrims bring back ZamZam water, dates, and rosaries, which they distribute among their relatives.

On the *aqiqa* ceremony of a newborn, a goat is sacrificed if the baby is a girl and two goats if the baby is a boy. As in Eid-ul-Azha, each animal sacrificed for the *aqiqa* is divided into three parts and distributed. The newborn's head is shaved and felicitations exchanged. The ceremony marking the child's first venture into reading is known as *Bismillah*. Observance of the occasion when the child completes his first reading of the Quran is called *Aameen*. Once that is done the child is deemed ready to travel towards the other goals in his life.

A third Eid observed in many Muslim countries celebrates the birth of the Prophet Mohammad (PBUH) on 12 Rabi-ul-Awwal of the Islamic calendar. People arrange for the *sabeel,* or distribution of a cool drink, on their streets. Food is also cooked and distributed among the poor. The *milad*, recounting the life and miracles of the Prophet, is read and celebrated in many homes and public places. At Data Sahib's mausoleum it is held daily for 12 days. Actually whenever there is a special occasion, like the wedding of one's child, a recitation of the Quran followed by a *milad* is organized. Educational institutions hold competitions in *naat* (poetry in praise of the Prophet) and *qirat* or melodic recitation of the Quran. These activities continue throughout Ramzan, in the month of Rabi-ul-Awwal, especially on the 12th of the month, and on many other religious occasions.

People who celebrate Shab-e-Baraat make a variety of halwas at home and distribute them. Children and young men explode firecrackers on their streets despite the government's ban. People have become easygoing, so, instead of cooking, they buy halwa and puri from vendors for their own families and as gifts to their children's in-laws. From 18 to 27 Rajab many households prepare food as oblation for the *koonda* ritual. Instead of the traditional sweet biscuit-like *tikya*, guests nowadays are served a regular meal. The *tikyas* for the oblation are kept separately. Puries, halwa, pulao and korma are cooked in many homes.

The Islamic year begins with the month of Muharram. During this month, people of the Shia sect, especially, recount and mourn the events of Karbala and the martyrdom of Hazrat Imam Husain, detailing the events of the ten days during which even children were denied water and remained thirsty. This heart-rending recitation is carried on at gatherings called *majlis*. These gatherings segregate men and women. Cool milk and sherbet is placed outside the venue of the *majlis*. Oblation food is distributed from large vessels. *Tazia, Alum,* and *Zuljinnah* processions take government-approved routes. Mourners recite *marsiyas, nohas,* and *salaam* as they lament and beat their breasts. They walk barefooted and many women join them in this. From the seventh to the tenth of Muharram, traditions such as beating themselves with chains and walking on fire are followed. All media channels arrange for sermons on the philosophy of martyrdom in the context of Hazrat Imam Husain.

Women who can afford it have special black outfits tailored for the first ten days of Muharram. During the course of the *majlises* many proposals of marriage are confirmed. On the ninth and tenth of Muharram members of both Shia and Sunni sects fast and distribute food among the poor. There are some distasteful practices, such as sending children dressed as Imam Husain's faqirs (or beggars) from house to house, collecting alms. Practices of this sort are on the way out. However, the memory of Hazrat Imam Husain will last as long as humanity exists.

The Hindu community celebrates Shoratari, Holi, Rakhsha Bandhan, Desehra, and Diwali. On these occasions people send sweetmeats and other presents to their friends and relatives. Christians fast for forty days before Easter, then observe Easter. They celebrate Christmas on 25 December. That is also the day when the whole nation celebrates the birthday of the Quaid-e-Azam with illuminations. On Independence day, 14 August, young men eject the silencer on their motorbikes and drive around singing national songs. On the official level the national flag is hoisted. All media channels broadcast nationalist songs. On 23 March the Pakistan Resolution Day (originally Lahore Resolution Day) is observed with extensive illuminations.

8

Our Sports

FROM THE VERY INCEPTION OF PAKISTAN, HOCKEY WAS declared the national sport of this country. Pakistan made its name worldwide in this sport. Naseer Banda, Islahuddin, Shehnaz Shaikh, Sameeullah, Hasan Sardar, and Shehbaz Ahmed earned so much fame on an international level, that the name of Pakistan became known all over the world. However, this glow of excellence has dimmed in the past few years and Pakistan now occupies only the eleventh position in the pecking order of the states that have produced the world's best hockey players. Meanwhile the other sport that earned a name for Pakistan among the nations of the world is cricket. India and Pakistan had their first cricket match in 1952. Among the first Pakistani cricket stars were Hafeez Kardar, Fazal Mehmood, Imtiaz Ahmed, Maqsood Ahmed, and more than all else, the 'Little Master' Hanif Mohammad, who created an extraordinary record of sixteen hours and ten minutes of steadfast batting in the longest Test innings, unbroken to this day.

In 1992 Pakistan once again made the headlines when, captained by Imran Khan, it won the World Cup. During this time Pakistani cricket found two exceptional cricketers in the form of Waseem Akram and Waqar Younus, who gave fast bowling new dimensions. Mohammad Yousuf created a new world record by making the highest number of runs in a single calendar year. Saqlain Mushtaq, Shoaib Akhtar, Inzimamul Haq, Sayeed Anwar, and Shahid Afridi gained world fame and established many records. Presently, Pakistan is number one in Test Cricket and number nine in One Day Cricket.

Pakistan's third most important sport is squash. It has won for Pakistan most of the international awards reserved for the game. The first Pakistani squash player to earn international fame was Roshan Khan. Then came Hashim Khan, Jahangir Khan, and Jan Sher Khan. Qamar Zaman and Gogi Alauddin also came to the fore but unfortunately, could not transform themselves into squash players of international standing.

In the year 2016, Pakistan won the International Championship. In the last few years Aisamul Haq has made a name in tennis. Women players have also gained significance in this sport. Saba Aziz was the first woman tennis player. Sania Malik and Sameed Malik also made a name in the country but were not able to make it to the international scene.

Rabia Ali Chaudhry and Asma Butt became national badminton champions. Omar Zeeshan, Rizwan Asghar, and Saima Manzoor are important badminton players. Sabiha Zahid became a famous cyclist.

Women's hockey and cricket teams also took part in international sports, and managed to earn fame. The team of blind cricket players even won international honours. A squash team of handicapped players is making a name in Pakistan.

Mohammad Yusuf won the World Championship in snooker. Naveen Perwani and Mohammad Asif also found fame. A young player Hamza Akbar created a world record. There is a National Chess Championship, but no Pakistani chess player has been able to make a name on an international level. Young Pakistani table tennis players, boys and girls, play on the international level. Every year there are national sports which include swimming, gymnastics, high jump, and other sports. Players from all government institutions including the army, banks and mobile companies take part in these. There are body building contests in all the provinces. Ice skating attracts even foreign tourists. Kabaddi is a game that is especially popular in Pakistani and Indian Punjab. There are Kabaddi contests between the two countries. Pakistan also became the Asian Champion in this sport. Boat races too are very popular in the two Punjabs. In Sindh, boating competitions are known as *mullakhara*. Polo is very popular in the army, and in the northern areas of Pakistan. Golf is much favoured by the rich, retired government officers, and members of the armed forces. Nowadays jeep races and donkey cart races are arranged each year. In villages, cock and dog fights are also popular.

At first the mountains were scaled only by foreign mountaineers. But now this sport has gained so much popularity that Samina Baig from Gilgit was able to climb the Everest. She was Pakistan's first woman mountaineer. Carrying luggage for mountaineers and acting as their guides is a source of livelihood for the people of this region. Young men and women train in Islamabad and mountainous areas to climb mountains. Nowadays computer games have gained a lot of popularity among children and adults. Presently a baseball stadium is being constructed.

Husain Shah is a boxer of world fame. Although football is a favourite sport all over the world it has not gained much popularity in Pakistan. However, the Baloch and the Makranis are excellent footballers and are very partial to the game. Kalimullah was the first Pakistani to play Professional Football in America. Similarly, Ice hockey has not been introduced in Pakistan. In the Malam Jabba region, local and foreign teams come to skate during the three coldest winter months. Sea sports are common in the world, but in Pakistan these sports have not gained traction. Swimming and boating are confined to universities, but seem to go no further. Archery attracts some. Table tennis is also mostly confined to universities; Pakistanis have not made a name in this sport on an international level. Handball is not very popular yet. Volleyball and badminton are played in our villages too.

Naseem Hameed won an international prize on winning the hundred metre race. Weight lifting is popular in Punjab. Forty years ago doing the dips, boxing, and bodybuilding were common and popular. Nowadays there are gyms in every town and city frequented by young men and women who wish to lose weight, or by young men desiring to build their bodies. Arm wrestling is another sport in which Pakistanis have done well, defeating India in many contests.

Parks in towns and cities have many kinds of swings for children. In the village there is no such facility, so the *jhulaiwala* goes from village to village with his small, portable Ferris wheel, attracting children who get a ride for a small amount of money.

In most of our urban and rural schools there is in the first place, no ground to speak of, and if there is, it is an untended piece of land with no semblance of a playground. Children are simply told to 'go out and play', but few schools have sports instructors who can direct their energy into organized sport. In our villages the favourite diversion of children is to climb trees and pluck raw mangoes.

Before they start school, children frequently play 'Ludo', and when they are a little older they might move on to cards. In every village, children are seen playing cricket, having put up some bricks to serve as a makeshift wicket. Children old or young play cricket wherever they find some space. In urban areas they are seen to play even in parking lots or on the less busy roads and streets. However, girls do not have recourse even to such improvised means of recreational pursuits.

There are only a few stadiums in the country, and the same is true of playgrounds. Unused or neglected land is grabbed by the land mafia. Unlike China or the US, no planning is undertaken in Pakistan for training future sportsmen or sportswomen.

9
Our Dress

FOR A WHILE BOTH BEFORE AND AFTER THE INCEPTION OF Pakistan, Quaid-e-Azam used to be attired sometimes in a sherwani and other times in a Western style suit. His sister, Fatima Jinnah, who used to accompany him, would wear a sari or a gharara. When Begum Rana Liaquat Ali Khan first visited the United States, she took with her ghararas specially stitched under the supervision of Begum Daulatana. Most women migrating to Pakistan from UP and CP wore either the gharara or the sari. Elderly women usually wore the *tang pajama*.

Bohri women in Sind usually wear burka of a different style from the norm—the top is round and the lower part of the garment comes down to the feet. A veil is not a part of this type of burka. Parsi women wear skirts or saris. They wear saris with the edge of the garment over their shoulder to the front (instead of the back as worn by other subcontinental women). Parsi men wear their traditional attire on weddings. It comprises of a toga or robe and a pagri. Pakistani Christians wear either the kameez shalwar like everybody else or trousers and tops, or skirts, and dresses. Bohri men wear a special round cap, long kurtas and pyjama and shoes. Women of the Hindu community wear the typical kurta and shalwar that is the attire of most Pakistani women. But on special occasions such as the Diwali they dress in a sari, or lehnga. Women of Tharparkar and Cholistan attire themselves in choli or short blouse, *ghagra* or long, pleated skirt, and a three yard long dupatta. Men from Tharparkar wear the usual Pakistani kameez and shalwar on most days, but on special days they wear a dhoti with the edge of the cloth tucked in at the back. Over this dhoti they wear a kurta and a colourful pagri or headgear. Married Tharri women wear bangles on their whole arms. Widowed, they can wear them only up to their elbows. 54 per cent of the population in Thar is Hindu. Since they do not eat meat, animals are not slaughtered there out of respect for the Hindu faith. Under Saudi and Iranian influence, the fashion for wearing a hijab has grown among Pakistani Muslim women.

In rural areas of Punjab elderly women commonly used to wear a black dhoti, white kurta, and dupatta. However, with changing times and circumstances they mostly wear shalwar, kurta, and dupatta. In every part of Pakistan, the tradition of covering the head is widespread among women and young girls. In the decades of the 50s and 60s schoolteachers in the Khyber Pakhtunkhwa and Punjab provinces used to wear the burka. Nowadays, whether it is Charsadda, Bahawalpur, or Khairpur, women and girls can be seen travelling in Ching-chi rickshaws with their faces and heads only half covered with a dupatta or chador.

However in the Bannu, Kark, and Mardan region Afghan women can be seen in blue and white burkas. In the large or small districts of Sind women can be seen in the marketplace with their face only half covered with their chadors. Women working in the fields, whether they are plucking cotton, planting rice, or digging up potatoes, have their heads covered. Similarly male workers, whether they are labourers or farmers, tie their own style of pagri on their heads especially in summer. The pagri is suitable for the weather they work in and is also a symbol of honour and respect for the wearer.

Fashion designers and the media have introduced not only townspeople but also villagers to new designs and fashions. Women and girls either buy readymade garments or go to tailors and choose designs from fashion magazines. Curiously enough, fashions that were popular in the 1960s, such as bellbottom pyjamas or trousers, high-heeled shoes, sleeveless kameezes, are back in vogue now. In the 60s decade, long kameezes and large bottoms of pyjama legs were in fashion. In the last four or five years, one can see in every street and neighbourhood, women wearing kameezes with their front and back of different designs. This fashion is still popular. City girls like to wear tight pyjamas with short kameezes.

The fame of some Pakistani designers has crossed the country's borders. They have fashion shows abroad, and people generally like their designs. Wedding fashions also keep changing. At first it was mandatory for a bride to be seen in a gharara. The *farshi gharara* then took the place of the simple gharara, which in time was superseded by the tight pyjama and Lucknavi kurta. Then came the kurta and sharara, now overtaken by the choli and sharara. Bridegrooms' fashions have also been changing. There have been changes in the design of the sherwani, but the sherwani itself never went out of fashion for the bridegroom, though the lower garment can be, interchangeably, *tang pyjama*, *Aligarh pyjama*, or shalwar. The bridegroom wears the Jodhpuri, Rajistani, or Sindhi pagri. On his feet, he wears the brightly embroidered *khussa*.

Women take to these fashions and adopt them when they see them on television. However, in most parts of Balochistan they have kept to their own style, which is, kurta, dupatta, and shalwar worked with Baloch embroidery (typically, the lower edges of the shalwar are also embroidered). Previously henna used to be applied at home by a family member. Now, professional henna appliers go from house to house. In urban areas girls go to beauty parlours to have henna applied to their hands, arms, and feet. The bridegroom also goes to a men's beauty parlour where he is given a facial. Earlier, men only wore white kurtas, but nowadays kurtas, and short shirts in every colour have come into vogue. Even in the villages a coloured, silken kurta worn with a dhoti and *khussa* is not an uncommon sight, especially at weddings.

Previously, the bride used to be taken from her home to the bridegroom's in a palanquin. Now she goes in a car, and not from her home but from a hotel or a 'Shaadi Hall'. In small town or village weddings the bridegroom arrives at the bride's home on a horse. Dancing the bhangra, his friends lead the wedding party. In the cities, bridegrooms from wealthy households arrive at the bride's house in a horse-drawn buggy, led by jubilant friends dancing the bhangra. In the past there used to be a Babu band in every town. It used to play film tunes as it led the wedding party. Then came the police band. Even now people arrange for a band, settling for one they can afford. Wearing a pagri is essential, whether in Fata or Balochistan. In Waziristan and Kohistan a white woollen cap is worn even in summer. In Khyber Pakhtunkhwa men wear a special cap called a *pakol*. People of other nationalities too have started wearing this cap, especially in winter.

Wealthy and fashionable women wear saris when they go to a wedding. In the small towns of Punjab a bride's trousseau is exhibited even now. The older daughters-in-law pick up each set of clothes and display it to the guests. In Balochistan and Khyber Pakhtunkhwa, the bridegroom has to pay for all the wedding expenses, including the trousseau. When Young Pakistanis who work in the Middle Eastern countries come home, they spend their money on weddings. If they have more, they use it to build a house. Usually little of it goes to educate children. A labourer returning from Dubai first buys the whole wish list for each member of his family. He then comes home for just one month.

Ten or fifteen years ago village guests in a wedding would eat the wedding meal sitting down, and facing each other. Now, food is catered everywhere. It is served in large platters and villagers eat sitting on rugs or the ground. In hotels buffets are more common.

In parts of Khyber Pakhtunkhwa and Balochistan, in southern Punjab, and in interior Sind some old rituals still exist. Examples of these are Vani, Swara, Badal-e-Sulah, and Sung chiti. Each of these ritualistic practices involves handing over a girl as the price for something. In many places an eight-year-old girl is given in marriage to a 75-year-old man in Badal-e-Sulah. In Kohat and Karak there is the tradition of Sar Paisa and Walwar. Girls in Bajor and Kohistan have made songs about such abusive treatment of women.

In Swabi and Hazara communities Pashtoon embroidery, mustard embroidery on a red sheet, and a tablecloth are essential items in the trousseau. In Balochistan as soon as a female child is born, suits of clothes with Baloch embroidery are prepared for her. Women, whether they come from rich or poor families, wear suits embroidered in the Baloch style. However, school and college going girls dress in conformity with modern fashions, in addition to the traditional attire.

Some wedding rituals limited earlier to a few communities or households have now become much more widespread, thanks to the media. Among these are *joota churai* (in which the bride's sisters 'steal' one of the bridegroom's shoes, and do not return it until he pays them a stipulated sum of money). Another popular wedding ritual is *kheer chataee*, in which the bridegroom is made to lick the kheer from the bride's hand. A movie of the wedding is almost de rigueur. It is made in every household even if the sexes are segregated.

In 1970 there was a change in men's attire. So far men had been wearing kameez shalwar at home, and trousers and shirt or Western style suits to the office. The change came when Zulfikar Ali Bhutto started the trend of wearing kameez and shalwar of the same material and colour. This was known as the Awami suit. It became so popular that orders for it came from India.

Thanks to Bhutto the Awami Suit became the official attire, and was worn by all—from poor labourers to ministers of state. The designers now got working. They embellished the kameez of the Awami suit and made them more expensive. With Zia ul-Haq a waistcoat was added to the outfit.

When men who had lived abroad returned to Pakistan, they continued to wear shorts in private as well as in public. Pakistani women were not far behind, and they adopted Western trends in clothes. Poor people got their Western clothes—T-shirts, trousers and shorts—from the second-hand market.

Cotton and silk fabrics of high quality are made in Pakistan. Cotton lawn is very popular among women because of the hot weather. It is much favoured by Indians as well. However, rich Pakistani women are partial to imported cloth.

All the different regions of Pakistan are known for their own special style of embroidery. The more prominent styles of embroidery are the Sindhi, Multani, Swati, and Balochi styles. With the arrival of the Afghans in Pakistan we have silk embroidery on men's and women's kurtas. These kurtas are usually made of silk fabric. Girls embroider bedcovers and pillowcases for their trousseau. It is interesting that girls in the Pashtun areas always embroider parrots on pillowcases, while Sindhi and Punjab girls embroider couplets from poetry. Every town known for its embroidery has its own special stitch.

The Sindhi *ajrak* and *rulli* are ubiquitous in Sindhi homes. Numerous *rullies* can be found in the poorest as well as richest of homes, hanging on the walls or spread on beds. It is customary for a girl to have at least six *rullies* in her trousseau. There are women skilled at cutting up the cloth into small pieces for the *rulli*, and other women who are equally skilled at joining the pieces together. Both the patchwork of the upper layer, and the lining are sewn by hand. However, increasingly, people now do the sewing by machine.

The real *ajrak* is prepared by dipping the fabric twelve times into different dyes. When ready, its price runs into thousands of rupees. Nowadays most *ajraks* are machine printed. They are draped on guests on special occasions. Some designers are creating women's suits, bedcovers, and pillowcases in *ajrak* designs. Hala and Thatta are known for block printing in natural colours. From Swat, cotton and wool shawls made on looms in Islamkot are exported. Items such as shoulder bags, purses, *rullies*, cushion covers, and pillowcases are made by women in Nagarparkar, Umerkot, and Mithi, and sold by their men in Karachi.

Thanks to the interest shown by foreign tourists, shops have opened in large cities of Pakistan which sell these objects, making large profits on them. *Putti khaddar* from Charsadda has an identity of its own. Waistcoats are made out of this fabric. Handloom fabric from Charsadda is very popular for men's suits. Handloom Banarsi silks from Khairpur are famous. In the villages of Badin and Bahawalpur *bandani* suits are made from both silk and cotton. Handloom silk from Hala and Islamkot is of excellent quality but is very expensive. Only the rich can afford to buy it. The common people wear khaddar made on machines in Kamalia. In Kamalia khaddar is made on handloom as well, but it is unsuitable for summer wear. Swabi and Bajor have their own distinctive stitch. Women's chadors with designs, are made here on mechanized looms. Men's shawls on looms are made in Charsadda and Bannu. In Jhang, khaddar cloth and rugs used to be made by women, but now they are made by men. Khaddar, or Khadi as it is now known, embellished with new designs and machine embroidery, is used to prepare either unstitched or readymade garments which are currently very much the fashion. They have converted Pakistani imported cloth enthusiasts to aficionados of locally produced textiles. Pakistani broad-cloth, and cotton fabric in other forms are exported. Pakistani women living in America and London send for ready-made and unstitched suits from Pakistan and hold exhibitions where they make good profits. Many of the suits they order are worked in gold and silver threads, suitable for wedding wear.

In Thatta, girls prepare embroidered wedding suits on wooden frames. In Kohat and Hinko women make mats, handheld fans, and straw baskets. In the villages of Qasoor, men and women make reed blinds, which, with new designs, have come into fashion in the cities as well. In short, with the exception of old people, no one in the poorer classes is unoccupied.

Multan's blue pottery is famous. Even foreign tourists now buy the blue kettles made in Peshawar for making tea. Table lamps, ashtrays, vases, and many other objects made from Baloch marble are very popular, and so are all kinds of decorative vessels in copper. Chiniot is known for furniture and other objects made with carved wood. Lampshades, purses, and bags made of camel skin come from Balochistan and Tharparkar.

10

Our Means of Communication

THE BULLOCK CARTS ONE SOMETIMES SEES IN FILMS USED TO bring people to the towns. With development, the bullock cart stayed in the villages, while urban centres got the *yakkah* or one-horse carriage. About six years later, the *tanga* made its appearance on city roads. It was seen ubiquitously in the cities of UP, CP, Punjab, Khyber Pakhtunkhwa, Sind, and Balochistan. The tanga driver charged 4 annas per passenger, or one rupee for the whole tanga. The villages had the bullock cart and the *yakkah*. Karachi had a local train, a tram service and the victoria. In those days roads in Karachi used to be washed. The donkey cart carried cargo in Karachi as well as in interior Sind and Punjab. Pakistan Western Railway served the length and breadth of (the then) West Pakistan.

Dakota planes plied the airspace between Delhi and Lahore from 1947 to 1950, transporting migrants from one country to the other. These airplanes came into use during World War II. Pakistan's airline then was Orient Airways, which was later renamed Pakistan International Airlines or PIA.

From 1948 buses were introduced. They had inter-city and intra-city routes. Tongas stood by to take passengers from city to village. Roads were not metalled and there were few schools. Gradually, girls who had completed their Matric began to start private primary schools. In the city of Lahore, young men from rich families took to driving their own bedecked tongas festooned with bells, on Mall Road. When the number of cars in the city increased, the traffic grew. Movement of tongas on Mall Road had to be restricted in the seventies. However, they still ply the roads outside the city centre.

The tonga is probably Pakistan's earliest means of public transport. It appears in the annals of Quetta, Peshawar, and Hyderabad Sind. The government of Pakistan started distributing rickshaws and taxis among the poor at reduced prices. To avoid paying the high price of petrol, rickshaw drivers fuelled their vehicles with gas from small gas cylinders which they placed in the rickshaw. In the eighties the Nawaz Sharif government put an end to cycle rickshaws in Bahawalpur and gave fuel-powered rickshaws to their owners, relieving them from the strain of pulling cycle rickshaws. However, even now, young and old men can be seen pulling carts full of iron rods, cement bags, and other loads, in every city. Furthermore, when a bus stops at an intercity bus station, ten- or twelve-year-old children can be seen waiting with small garbage carts to carry the passengers' luggage. Children who do not have a cart carry the passenger's luggage on their heads. Such scenes of child labour can be seen in every city.

The population of Pakistan is growing at a high speed. Villagers are moving to cities in search of work. This trend has resulted in the growth of squatter settlements in cities. Problems of health care, education, and other civic issues have proliferated. At first people had added seats to their motor bikes and turned them into rickshaws. Later the Chung Chi was imported from China, which could seat four to six passengers. Mini buses ply the streets of every city. Women are usually allocated the front seats, while young men frequently accommodate themselves on the roof of the bus.

Nowadays inter-city buses are air-conditioned. There are buses which stop at no more than two or three places before they bring their passengers to Karachi. Air-conditioned buses also link other cities.

The railway in Pakistan worked very well until 1980. In those days trains plied between Karachi and Lahore, Rawalpindi, Faisalabad, Multan, Sukkhar, Quetta, Peshawar, Sialkot. They had pretty names like, Tezgam, Shaheen Express, Tez Row, Subuk Raftaar, Subuk Kharam, Shalimar Express, etc. A Night Coach was started and has been travelling to and back from Lahore for the past twenty or twenty-five years. Once again there is talk of developing the railway. However, there seems to be a slide in the fortunes of the railway in Pakistan. Passenger carriages were sent for from China but became unusable in a few months. This experiment was repeated several times, only to meet the same end. The railway train was the only means of long distance transport for the poor and the lower middle classes. Railway tracks and trains were blown up by terrorists. However, people managed to travel somehow.

Pakistanis working in the Middle East often come home on a

month's leave in Ramzan. Or they might return to spend the Haj holidays in their homeland. A large number of Pakistanis work in the Middle East, especially in Saudi Arabia and the UAE. Working extremely hard, they send home foreign currency, thus contributing to the development of this country. Similarly Pakistanis living in Europe and America (who usually live there with their families) come to Pakistan during their children's school holidays. Most expatriate Pakistanis prefer to travel by PIA and regard this airline as their home where they are served Pakistani food.

Besides PIA, Air Blue and Shaheen International also offer domestic and international service to commuters. Emirates Airline has resumed its flights to Pakistan. In the days before terrorism blighted our land, British Airways and other international airlines used to operate flights to our country. Nowadays Qatar Airways and Turkish Airlines are among the few that have continued their flights to Pakistan. PIA has 38 planes at present. Efforts are being made to expand this fleet.

In 1946, realizing that an airline would be a necessity for Pakistan (there were to be an East and a West Pakistan, separated by 1600 km), Quaid-e-Azam asked rich Muslim businessmen to start an airline for the new country. This airline came to be known as Orient Airways. It started off with three Douglas DC-3 aircraft, with which it did relief operations for Pakistan during the Partition period. In 1955, it was renamed Pakistan International Airlines or PIA.

PIA enjoyed its most successful period, financially and

operationally, under the two terms of Nur Khan. For some years now, overburdened by corruption and overstaffing, PIA has been sustaining losses. At first, Pakistan had airports only in Karachi and Lahore. Later, airports were built in Islamabad, Multan, Hyderabad, Gilgit, Skardu, and Mohenjo-Daro; and then in Gwader and Turbat. Airports at Chitral and Muzaffarabad are used rarely, when the weather permits. The Dera Ismail Khan airport is used no more than once or twice a month. Liaquat Ali Khan Airport, a new airport is under construction in Islamabad. It is due to be opened in 2017.

Nowadays large companies and political parties also own planes. Flight training for pilots is given in Karachi, Lahore and Islamabad. There are several trained women pilots in PIA as well as in the Pakistan Air Force.

At the inception of Pakistan there were no roads in most of Balochistan. Donkeys were used for transportation. In interior Sind donkey carts are still used to transport loads. Taxis have now become common everywhere in Pakistan. For the last five or six years a few women taxi and rickshaw drivers have also emerged. Since last year some women have started driving trucks, and riding motorbikes. Up to 1960 many girls used to ride bicycles to college. Since then there have been buses. Many colleges and universities today have their own buses, yet they cannot accommodate all the college and university students who therefore have a hard time commuting to their educational institutions. A bus for student commuters to take them to their educational institution is a facility not available in rural areas. Because there is only a primary school in their own area, numerous boys and girls have to walk several kilometers to get to high school. Handicapped government servants are provided special transportation on a quota system.

The 'kekra' (crab) is used for transport in Tharparkar. Actually this vehicle is a truck dating from the Second World War period. It is known as a 'kekra' owing to its outspread wheels. A long plank attached to the back of a tractor engine offers seating or standing space for up to fifty commuters. There are roads in some parts of Tharparkar, but most of the area is desert or wasteland and uneven, so that only four wheelers or kekras can operate there.

In Khyber Pakhtunkhwa tongas, rickshaws, and taxis are common. The Suzuki van is used for short distances. In Sind, including Karachi, and northern and southern Punjab the Chung Chi is found to be cheaper and more appropriate for common travelers. Most villages have link roads which are traversable for tongas and rickshaws.

However, the bicycle is what most poor people use. There was a time when boys were given a bicycle after they had done their matric. But now children are given motorbikes even before they have sat for their Matric exam.

Apart from the railways, trucks are the only means for transporting cargo. Truck drivers eat at their special truck stations. They have a particular menu—*qorma* made of goat meat, *mahsh* lentils with ghee, and strong tea. Their breakfast consists of baked parathas, omelette, and a yogurt drink. Truck drivers sit on charpoys provided to them where they eat. After their meal, they lie down in the same place for a bit, and then resume their journey.

Until 1977 they could cross the Khyber Pass, get their visa, and travel to Kabul without any hindrance. But then came the Russian armed forces. When they left, those who were known as Mujahideen turned into terrorists. The Durand Line agreement was ignored or considered ended. Afghans travelled back and forth from Pakistan, unchecked. This was the root of terrorism. Pakistan was building a wall on the border. Afghanistan was annoyed. The border wall was abandoned for various reasons. However, the Pakistan Army completed a 1100 km long trench along the Pak Afghan border in June 2016. The position now, is that there are fewer hubs of militants in Pakistan but Afghanistan is their main centre of activity.

Lahore and Islamabad have metro busses, which have made good transport cheaper for the common man there. Multan, Karachi, and some other cities too are to be provided with a Metro Bus system.

In some parts of Azad Kashmir the river can be crossed in a cable trolley. There are bridges in other areas. Buses and taxis are available. Kohistan has a difficult terrain for transport. The mountainous road makes it difficult to communicate even with the towns. Shangla has lived through many earthquakes, and the consequent destruction.

A motorway was completed between Islamabad and Lahore in

the year 1997. Later it was expanded joining Peshawar to the network. The other provinces are also being linked in this way. Now the China Pakistan Economic Corridor (CPEC) project is being built to link the Gwader Port to Kashgar in China. On its completion, this project is expected to bring economic prosperity to all the provinces of Pakistan.

11

Our Women

BEFORE THE BIRTH OF PAKISTAN, ROUND TABLE CONFERENCES had been convened in London to bring about constitutional reforms in India which would satisfy the Indians and at the same time be found workable by the British. At these conferences Muslim women were represented by Begum Shahnawaz and Miss Fatima Jinnah. Fortunately for the women of Pakistan, they received full suffrage at the very inception of the country, in 1947. Therefore, unlike in the United States, Pakistani women did not have to struggle for their right to vote.

With enormous numbers of refugees pouring into Pakistan at Partition, a great deal of organization was needed to accommodate them and provide them with basic necessities. Begum Salma Tasadduq Husain, Begum G.A. Khan and other prominent women of Punjab undertook the responsibility of helping female refugees settle into their new homeland. In Karachi the same work was done under the direction of Lady Hidayatullah. However, it was Miss Fatima Jinnah and Begum Liaquat Ali Khan who assumed the main responsibilities.

Begum G.A. Khan organized Girl Guides throughout the province of Punjab. Begum Liaquat Ali Khan first organized

102

the Women's National Guards, and then created the All Pakistan Women's Association (APWA), which works in cooperation with social welfare societies in every district of Pakistan even today.

With the death of Quaid-e-Azam and the assassination of Liaquat Ali Khan, the bureaucrats became very powerful in Pakistan. Prime Ministers changed frequently. Mohammed Ali Bogra who had been Pakistan's ambassador in the United States was recalled and made Prime Minister of Pakistan. Bogra was a married man, but he took a second wife. His polygamy became the cause of a strong protest among privileged Pakistani women, who walked from Lahore to Rawalpindi to show their displeasure. In 1961 the Family Laws Ordinance was promulgated. Following this, women were given the right to inherit and own agricultural land. A man could take a second wife only with the permission of his first wife. Divorce was made difficult for the husband. For the first time women were given the right to seek *khula*, that is, a divorce initiated by the wife. The system of registering marriages was initiated. These developments did have a salutary effect in urban areas in matters such as marital disputes leading to divorce, child support, maintenance, and payment of *meher* or dower in the event of a divorce. Arbitration Councils were introduced.

Under Ayub Khan's Union Council system marriage registration and arbitration councils were initiated in rural areas as well, and the minimum age for marriage was fixed at 16 for girls and 18 for boys. However, governments changed from martial law to civilian, and then martial law again. Meanwhile, quite unmindful of the laws, village girls as young as 8 years continued to be given in marriage to old men nearing their eighth decade, for a sum of money or in settlement of a dispute. This practice has continued till the present day. It is not unusual to put down the age of a 10-year-old girl as 16. However, there are signs of an awakening conscience among men, for such occurrences do get reported to the police sometimes, and on equally infrequent occasions the police do take action.

Ayub Khan's martial law was followed by Yahya Khan's martial law. East Pakistan became Bangladesh. Zia ul-Haq ended Bhutto's government with yet another martial law. Under Zia's rule the central role of women ambassadors in their domain was reduced to a secondary one; artistes and female newscasters on television were obliged to cover their heads; sleeves appeared on Madam Noorjahan's sleeveless blouses; women who were the victims of rape were locked up in prison without any proof of guilt; under the law of evidence the evidence provided by a woman was downgraded to only half the value of evidence provided by a man and the murderer of a woman needed to pay only half of the blood money that the murderer of a man had to pay. New ordinances, responsible for such changes, infuriated women. The Women's Action Forum (WAF) was established, first in Karachi, then in Lahore, and lastly in Islamabad. Protests were organized. In order to awaken the conscience of Pakistanis, and the world, strong protests were arranged. On 12 February 1983, Habib Jalib stood in Regal Chowk and read his poem. The police, men and women, beat the protesting women so hard that half of them had to be taken to hospital while the other half found themselves in prison. WAF protested not sending the women's hockey team to play abroad, they protested against making a separate university for women, and against clamping restrictions on the media. WAF also campaigned against religious prejudice, and introducing a separate column for religion in the passport. Journalists, lawyers, associations of progressive students joined the movement.

Meanwhile, not heeding the insistence of world powers, Zia executed Zulfikar Ali Bhutto. The ex-prime minister of Pakistan was hanged at 2 a.m. on 4 July 1979, and buried in Garhi Khuda Bakhsh at 4 a.m. On 17 August 1988, after the airplane crash that killed Zia ul-Haq, Benazir Bhutto became the first woman Prime Minister of a Muslim country.

Under Benazir, some of the parliamentary seats taken away from women were restored. Courses in small industries were introduced for women. Women's police stations, and crisis centres for battered or persecuted women were established. Asma Jahangir built a shelter or *Dastak gah* for women. Every month surety was arranged for those women for whom nobody was willing to stand surety. However, Benazir's government lasted hardly two years. She was succeeded by Nawaz Sharif. During his term in office women appearing in dramas were charged not to let their dupattas slip from their heads, it was enjoined upon men and women that they should not be seen sitting on the same bed unless it was proved that they were husband and wife.

Benazir's second premiership again lasted two years, and once again it was succeeded by a Nawaz Sharif government. The political turmoil was such that General Pervaiz Musharraf ousted Sharif and established martial law in the country once again.

Local Bodies elections were held in which 33 per cent seats were reserved for women. Nawaz Sharif, who had been imprisoned, was sent to Saudi Arabia for eight years, and Benazir was barred from coming to Pakistan. A 33 per cent representation of women in the local bodies and parliament turned even several village women into politicians. For the next elections Benazir came to Pakistan despite Musharraf's ban. On 27 December 2007, at the end of a meeting with her supporters in Liaquat Bagh, when she stood up in her armoured vehicle to wave to the people, she was attacked by a gunman and fell unconscious. Almost immediately after, a suicide bomber detonated a bomb, killing 20 people. Benazir Bhutto was buried in Garhi Khudabakhsh. In accordance with her will, her son Bilawal was named Chairperson of the People's Party and her husband Asif Zardari was made Co-Chairperson. In the parliament, the number of women who subsequently became members was not 33 but 17 per cent. Four or five of them were elected directly and the rest nominated.

A National Commission on the Status of Women Ordinance was passed in 2000. It was replaced by the National Commission on the Status of Women Bill 2012 which strengthened the ordinance by giving it autonomy. A law was passed against violence on women. There is a resolution against acid attacks on women which has passed into law.

Many incidents of honour killing, and *karo kari* happen in Balochistan and southern Punjab. The percentage of literacy among women is 21% lower than among men. In rural girls' schools there is no washroom for girls and only a few of these schools have a boundary wall while one of five union councils has a high school for girls. The birth of a girl child is still not considered a good omen. However, in large cities and universities the percentage of female students is more than 70%.

The International Women's Day is observed on 8 March. On this day biased laws relating to women made during the year are reviewed. Under pressure from the United Nations, the Government of Pakistan accepted CEDAW (Convention on the Elimination of all Forms of Discrimination Against Women), barring a few of its articles. Nevertheless, no political party has mentioned in its manifesto the extent of representation it would allow to women in the Assembly and in the Union Council.

The Jirga system is still prevalent in all the tribal areas. In many regions religious societies have established religious reconciliation committees which make their own pronouncements, quite independently. In interior Sind compulsion in religious matters was attempted. The government and civil society reined in such coercion. However, it is not uncommon to take the law into one's own hand and kill the non-compliant man or woman.

Tahira Mazhar Ali established the Democratic Women's Association to help poor women, and wives and daughters of railway workers. As long as she was in good health, she served women in this way. In Karachi Kaneez Fatima was an active labour leader.

On 12 February 1983, there was a peaceful women's protest against Zia ul-Haq's discriminatory Law of Evidence. The protestors were lathi-charged and tear-gassed, while many were arrested. In memory of this protest 12 February 1983 is observed as Pakistan's Women's Day throughout the country.

Asma Jahangir and Hina Jilani started AGHS, a free legal aid centre, to help brick kiln workers and families as well as women with family issues such as divorce, custody of children, maintenance and alimony. In Karachi, Rasheeda Patel did the same for the women of Sind. Similarly, women lawyers in practically every city of Pakistan voluntarily help women with their problems. In addition several male lawyers, such as the late Senator Iqbal Haider and Barrister Aitezaz Ahson worked in cooperation with the women lawyers. However, despite these efforts there is no substantial reduction in heinous crimes such as throwing acid on women, honour killings, forced marriages, setting a woman on fire for bringing to her husband's home a smaller trousseau than that expected by the new family. Only one third of the women members in the Assemblies take part in debates throughout a session. The rest are happy and content to simply collect their honorarium, which is now thrice as much as before. This happens in spite of the training programmes groups such as the UNDP keep organizing for them.

The First Women's Bank, established in Benazir Bhutto's first term, was not able to help women significantly. Its first President was Akram Khatoon. Similarly, Benazir Bhutto's Income Support Programme has not been able to make women financially independent so far. However, in the past five years or so USAID has made some good programmes aimed at making women economically independent. However, they have not yet yielded significant results.

Faiz's wife, Alys Faiz, was among other things, a journalist. She wrote about women and children's issues for *Pakistan Times*, and was a human rights activist. Alys Faiz and Mariam Habib started a women journalists' association. When a newspaper fired a woman journalist, all the women not only resigned, they started the magazine *Newsline*. Razia Bhatti was the founding editor of this magazine. Pakistani women made a name for themselves in the electronic media. 50% of the anchors and reporters for television are women. Sultana Siddiqui resigned from PTV and started the Hum channel.

Women's universities were established in Islamabad and Quetta. Surveys show that they have been extremely helpful in providing higher education to girls from far-flung areas. In the year 1983 establishment of NGOs began. It does appear that there has been more social progress in small towns compared to big cities. Young girls have acquired a greater sense of responsibility and in the fields of health and education girls in the far-flung villages have done a good deal of work. Now boards proclaiming 'English Medium School' can be seen even in villages.

I.A.Rehman, Asma Jahangir, and Shehla Zia worked with much perseverance and diligence to establish the Human Rights Commission. The organization has a reputation for dependability, so much so that the world's news agencies have confidence in the information collected by it. The Federal government too has now established a Human Rights Commission.

Women's literacy in Balochistan is only 23 per cent. Owing to the presence of Khans, Sardars, and big landowners, there are very few schools, and a low percentage of literacy in the Kech and Khuzdar districts of Balochistan.

In Gwader, Abdullah Khadim Husain taught girls to teach in schools, bake buns, and make fish sandwiches. Many girls are now into making buns, with the permission of their mothers. Most mothers clean the fish and work so hard at it that many of them even lose their nails!

Even before Partition, Punjab had institutions like the Punjab University, and the Government College Lahore where there was co-education. In Lahore the percentage of girl students is 70 per cent, while male students lag behind. In higher institutions of industrial and computer training, girls too, are getting ahead. In the agricultural universities of Faisalabad, Tando Jam, and Peshawar, the percentage of female students equals that of male students. Similarly, in the fields of engineering and medicine, despite the fact that there are many separate girls' and boys' colleges, co-education is common.

Footballs handmade by women in the industrial city of Sialkot were used in the last World Cup. Children used to be part of the labour in the manufacture of the footballs, but ever since the international prohibition on child labour, the inclusion of children in the workforce has been discontinued. In Sialkot, a large number of girls also work in the medical tool-making industry.

Girls study in veterinary colleges and universities or veterinary departments of universities. In Tharparkar as well as other places there are women veterinary doctors. There is a veterinary university in every province of Pakistan, and it offers co-education.

Middle class Pakistani women work in the army, police, and rangers. They also work as airhostesses in passenger planes. Although there are vocational centres, their practical benefits are few. However, both educated and uneducated women run beauty parlours, whether working from home or from hired premises. Surveys show that beauty parlour training is very popular even in the villages.

Another important profession adopted by many Pakistani women is midwifery. In cities where the training is available, trained women open their own mother and child centres. In villages, women who are mostly untrained but have the experience, handle deliveries in the home of the mother-to-be. When there are complications the patient is rushed to the nearest hospital or dispensary. Mortality rates in such cases are high.

Prostitution, the 'oldest profession in the world' was outlawed in Pakistan in the year 1967 therefore no statistics are available on it, although the profession continues to exist.

Earlier, women were not acknowledged as agricultural workers. However, when women themselves asserted that they handle numerous stages of agricultural production, from planting rice seedlings to plucking cotton from the cotton plant, they were finally given international recognition for their work in agriculture.

Catering food to consumers directly from home and taking orders and supplying shops with sandwiches, kebabs, cakes, etc. is now very common. So much so that it has now become quite easy to order cooked meals on the phone. Most of this growing industry is operated by women.

Another field in which women are making a name internationally (although there are also many men in it) is designing. Many women have small businesses like stalls in Sunday bazaars where they sell anything from clothes, fashion accessories and other articles of use to women, to all kinds of plastics, and snacks like *pakoras* and *chaat*. Women also operate most of the stalls in town or country fairs.

Despite all these successful ventures and despite the fact that often they work for as long as 18 hours a day in the villages, there are women in parts of Khyber Pakhtunkhwa and Balochistan who are given neither identity cards, nor the right to vote. Often in the homes of big landowners, women are expected to do so much embroidery in return for just their meals, that eventually their eyesight is ruined.

Men pushing handcarts, from which they sell a variety of food, from *gol guppas* to *murgh cholas* or biryani, are a common sight on city, town and village streets. All these items of food are however prepared at home and are the products of women's labour. Watching female chefs conduct cooking sessions on television, inspires many young, educated women to take cooking courses and open their own restaurants. Another field in which both men and women are increasingly involved, is that of event management. Children's readymade clothes are stitched by women either at home or in factories. The remuneration in either case is generally very low. There are organizations such as the Kashf Foundation, NRSP (National Rural Support Program), and Akhuwat Foundation which are endeavouring to make men and women economically independent.

There was a time when women lawyers used to be a tiny minority in the legal profession. However, now there are women lawyers in every district. In many districts there are even women magistrates. As a member of the Election Commission, a woman, Irshad Bibi, was made a judge. This happened for the first time in Pakistan's history. Nasira Iqbal, a judge of the Lahore High Court, and Barrister Shahida Jameel also made their names in the legal profession.

Yasmeen Lari and Yasmeen Cheema are Pakistan's first women architects. Shama Usman was the Chairperson of Pakistan Council of Architects and Town Planners. Fawzia Quraishi, Sajida Vandal, and Shahnaz Arshad are also renowned Pakistani women architects.

There is one whole segment of women workers, rarely mentioned as professionals, who work in private houses. They are the domestic female labour that is responsible for sweeping and cleaning homes, washing and ironing, and cooking. Girls, even as young as eight or nine years old, are seen to carry their employer's children about, look after them and see to their every need. These members of the child labour force are treated at best with indifference, and at worst with great harshness.

Now we come to another area of women's activities which I am rather reluctant to touch upon; however it is part of the current scene. There are women who specialize in teaching the Quran and explaining its meaning. Farhat Hashmi is the fountainhead of this new expertise and profession.

Apart from this legitimate religious profession, there are others such as the one in which women have drawn their inspiration from male *aamils* and ersatz *pirs*. Such women now work through the computer, claiming to grant people their wishes through spiritual means, and in the process, earn a name and fortune for themselves.

Arranging marriages is yet another field of expertise which many women have now adopted as their profession. The day women get rid of their mental bondage to men and learn to make their own decisions, our culture will change.

12

Our Men

AT THE TIME OF PARTITION, THE POPULATION OF WOMEN WAS lower than the population of men. During the riots and relocation of populations, craftsmen tended to converge in one place. For example those who wove fabric on a loom, made furniture, specialized in painting furniture legs, etc. worked in one locality. Those who did not practise a craft worked as unskilled laborers. Educated people worked in offices, factories, banks, etc. As times changed many young people were drawn to going abroad for higher education and studying subjects like computer training. On the other hand, more than half of the population that lives in villages had to (and has to) find its livelihood within this country, as well as provide food for all the people of Pakistan. Many young men, scions of landowning families, came back with degrees in agriculture from universities abroad. However, owing to their privileged backgrounds and consequent predilection for luxurious living, although they did use their knowledge to grow new strands of wheat and rice, they did nothing to improve the lot of bonded and other poverty-stricken labour that had been working on their fields for generations.

Five hundred thousand Pakistani women are involved in cotton picking. In 2016 the cotton crop was damaged, and as a result their income dropped steeply. Such losses hit small farmers and farmhands the hardest.

In Pakistan, the average age of women is 69.8 years, and the average age of men is 65.8 years. Every year 299 out of every 100,000 women die in childbirth. According to 2013–14 data, 29.5% Pakistanis live under the poverty line.

Literacy rate among men in FATA is 45%, while among the women of FATA it is only 8%. The overall literacy rate for 2012–13 in Pakistan was 58%. With this low rate Pakistan is very likely to miss the United Nations' Millennium Development Goals under which Pakistan was required to have a literacy rate of 88% by 2015.

On an average, one hospital bed is available for 1,613 patients. Unemployment is at its highest in southern Punjab and Balochistan. Layoffs in the Gulf countries have an effect on overall income here. 3,000,000 people are unemployed in Pakistan, because there are no new opportunities of earning a livelihood, such as are offered by a country with a dynamic industrial growth.

A good deal of drug and human smuggling goes on in Pakistan. As in some other countries, smuggling of heroin, which also employs women, is carried out on a professional level. In the last approximately 25 years, target killings, terrorism, and extortions have become among the chief banes of public life.

In the last twenty years work related to computers has become popular among young people. The mobile phone industry has proliferated in the cities. Repairing laptops, computers, and mobile phones is work that even scantily educated youth take up for a living. Similarly, thanks to a booming population and a surge in the demand for transport, driving rickshaws and taxis has become an important source of income.

Pedagogy is a respected profession for both men and women in cities as well as rural areas. Schools, coaching, tuition, and language centres offer employment opportunities to educated youth. Motor workshops abound, often set up by talented but uneducated entrepreneurs, and employing untutored workhands.

Karachi being a port city, and the home of Pakistan Navy, has opportunities for service and employment in all areas of work linked to ships and shipping. Similarly, trained people work in Civil Aviation. The Army attracts most young men. They have ended terrorism in Waziristan. Different segments of the army have helped the country in defending it as well as in times of trouble such as the floods. Urban security and firefighting too are manned by young men, yet there are not enough jobs.

The largest social service organization is the Edhi Foundation. Its founder, Abdus Sattar Edhi died in July 2016. Edhi established Emergency Centres in all the districts of Pakistan. Women work with men in all the main offices. There are other organizations which work in the style set by Sattar Edhi. Then, in many towns and cities individuals arrange lunch and dinner for the common people who can get a meal for as little as 3 to 10 rupees. In Karachi and Lahore such eating places are run on donations.

Common citizens need to be familiarized with their basic responsibilities such as keeping roads clean, waiting in queues for their turn to climb into a bus or train, getting children inoculated, treating women politely, voting, and allowing women to vote as well as getting identity cards. People should be repeatedly reminded of these civic duties by the media and the NGOs, but this is not done.

If men, who are the main driving force in our culture, facilitate change for the better, planning can be successful, poverty reduced, violence to women ended, and Pakistan can become a prosperous and peaceful country.

Sending matriculated young men abroad is all the rage in rural areas. Some hiring countries have stipulated that aspiring candidates learn their language and are trained for their job. If these conditions are not satisfied, employers in the Middle East tend to confiscate the passports of their newcomer employees or even tear them up. They make their employees work extremely hard and because they are not registered workers, these recruits are paid the smallest wage.

Most people think that government jobs are secure. So, even a young man with a Master's degree could apply for a job as a peon in a government office, or a soldier in the Army. Young men with high educational degrees, often obtained abroad, are able to find good jobs thanks to the many multinationals that have opened their offices in Pakistan. Salaries have gone up in the Civil Service as well. Since government schools do not have enough seats to offer all the children, there are more private schools than state schools, where there are both male and female teachers. Five thousand schools in Balochistan are located in just one room.

Young men hailing from the area between Jehlum and Peshawar prefer to go into the army. Those with high educational degrees in electronics often join the Pakistan Air Force, or work in aeronautical companies at home or abroad. The naval workforce is also preponderantly male. Many businessmen have moved their organizations abroad owing to the atmosphere of political instability and terrorism currently prevailing in Pakistan. However, male labour still fills sugarcane crushing and cotton ginning factories in Pakistan. Cement manufacturing and the construction industry are flourishing and the architectural sector, linked to them, is growing, like Information Technology.

As in other international centres, there is ongoing research in medical sciences including psychology. Dr Abdus Salam had received the Nobel Prize for his research in Physics.

In Pakistan one can see hundreds of men, young and old, lining the roads with their shovels, spades, or tools for house or furniture painting, awaiting someone who will give them work on a daily wage. Small traders who depend for their living on an indefinite daily income park their handcarts in front of offices, selling roasted sweet potato, water chestnuts, peanuts, or corn on the cob. The men who bake *naans* or chapattis work from morning to night. Labour, working on making buildings or roads is dominated by men but sometimes includes women.

Mine workers have the longest and harshest working hours. Sometimes their work even proves fatal. Similarly many workers are electrocuted because they work on an electrical pylon without taking proper protective measures. Other workers die of asphyxiation when cleaning a gutter because of poisonous gases that have accumulated there. In most poverty-stricken homes there is usually no more than one earning member in a family of eight. When they are ill it is not the medical doctor they seek, but the charm and talisman seller, or the alternate faith healer.

From Sir Syed Ahmed to Quaid-e-Azam, it was men who successfully worked to awaken Muslims to their needs and responsibilities. From Allama Iqbal to Faiz Ahmed Faiz men wrote poetry to stimulate their love for their people, and their awareness. The present times also demand well-informed people with the right talents to come forward and lead the people.

13

Our Basic Rights

AT THE INCEPTION OF PAKISTAN, MEMBERS OF ALL SOCIAL classes, religions, races, and sects, were promised equal rights, without discrimination on the basis of gender or fortune. The present Constitution of Pakistan stipulates that no member of the minorities and no woman can be nominated or elected President of Pakistan, while no member of the minorities can become Prime Minister. However, women can be elected for all offices, excepting President. Pakistan is the only Muslim country where a woman, Benazir Bhutto, was twice elected Prime Minister with the consensus of the Parliament and the public. As is borne out by the Pakistan flag as well, a fourth of all seats in every organization must be reserved for minorities. However, this is not done.

The first Constitution of Pakistan was made in 1956. But the second Constitution of Pakistan was prepared in 1973 under Zulfikar Ali Bhutto with the support of all the political parties, including the Opposition. Pakistan was given the name of 'Islamic Republic of Pakistan'. Under this Constitution women were given the opportunity to serve as ambassadors of Pakistan, and non-civil service men and women were given 33 per cent postings. Women were given 10 per cent seats in the National and Provincial Assemblies. Members were given posts according to merit, at all positions. In 1976, in a storm of political upheaval Bhutto declared the Ahmedis a minority, announced Friday the weekly holiday, instead of Sunday, prohibited alcohol, and removed all Ahmedis from important posts in the country. Rigging at the polls became the justification for Martial Law imposed by Zia ul-Haq who imprisoned Bhutto along with the leaders of all the political parties.

Ayub Khan had already ended journalistic freedom. Under Zia-ul-Haq even section officers of the Ministry of Information could censor news items, columns, and pictures in newspapers. A journalist, or any other individual, who spoke against the government was given twenty lashes as punishment for his 'crime'. Under the Hudood Ordinances, women who were raped were put in prison, since four witnesses to the rape could not be found to prove that the woman had been forced. Under Zia ul-Haq also, in financial matters the evidence of one male witness was declared equal to that of two women. Under the law of Diyat if the compensation for the murder of a woman is Rs. 50,000, then that for slaying a man is Rs. 1,00000 which is twice that for a woman. These laws cannot be challenged in any court. Incarceration and lashes were declared punishment for the inebriated. All these bylaws were given the name of 'Eighth Amendment' and became laws.

Under the Human Rights Commission the court could be moved for forced labour. Similarly, sexual abuse of children and forced child labour are illegal. The minimum age of marriage is 16 years for a girl and 18 years for a boy.

Under Ayub Khan only tea could be served at a wedding, and the girl's trousseau could not be displayed. With the end of Ayub Khan's government these rules were scrapped. Later Nawaz Sharif put a restriction on all food provided at a wedding, unless it was served at home. Subsequently 'one dish' was allowed in all hotels.

In the area of agriculture the percentage of landless farmers is almost 40. They work as tenant cultivators and receive the eighth part of a crop. Usually these people spend this income on their children's weddings. Most of the time poor tenant farmers borrow money on high interest and spend the rest of their lives paying off their debts. Under British rule well-wishers of the government were given acres of land. According to the Hari Report there was an attempt to withdraw the dispensation, but such endeavours could not get past the powerful lobby of landowners and *vaderas* populating the Assemblies. In every budget benefits are announced for small farmers but the rich landlords in the Assemblies did not wish to give the farmers and landless peasants their rights. It is said about the Chief Minister of Punjab, Ghulam Haider Wyne, that he was slain as a consequence of his struggle for the rights of the common man. Every few years there are floods in the rainy season which drown whatever savings the farm labourers may have managed to accumulate.

Minority rights are the same as the rights of Muslims. Young men from among the minorities occupy positions in the government and private sectors according to their merit. Marriage and divorce laws for Hindus and Christians are still being debated in Parliament. Recently a law was passed on the rights of eunuchs. But even now there is dispute over post mortems of a eunuch, as well as over offering funeral prayers for a eunuch.

Even though Pakistanis are not as intensely aware of caste as are Hindus next door, yet most people prefer to marry within their own families or castes. The media has been attempting to raise awareness of the fact that marrying close relatives increases the possibility of Thalassemia in the offspring.

Even though men and women are equal under the law, when it comes to getting an identity or a health card, or even voting, women are not treated equally with men. Many girls are not taken through the whole protective inoculation cycle. Daughters are deprived of their rightful share of inheritance despite the fact that they are authorized to receive it by Quranic as well as by statute law. A girl who wants her legal inheritance either ends up fighting her case all her life or is sometimes killed to shorten the dispute, if she proves to be too troublesome. The excuse given by families is that girls receive a valuable trousseau. It is important for both boys and girls to have identification cards at the time of their wedding. However, this is not particularly followed.

A chapter on human rights should be mandatory from Class 4 onwards. Among other things, it should teach the rules for walking on the road, traffic rules, and the importance of observing all those rules. It should also teach children that when lining up for a bus the elderly should not only be allowed to climb up first but should also be assisted. The traffic police as well as everyone else should help the handicapped. Information on polio immunization should be part of the school curriculum. Children should be instructed to visit and take fruit for sick people in hospitals on holidays. They should also volunteer in social service organizations like the one owned by Abdul Sattar Edhi. They should be taught to respect their elders, greet them with an *Assalam alaikum* on waking up in the morning, and say *Shab Bakhair* to them before going to bed at night.

There is a commission for children which liberates them from enslavement and releases them from jails. Yet children often work in restaurants and other eateries. They work as labourers and even as domestic servants. Many children are kidnapped and trained to become suicide bombers. Some of the child suicide bombers have been known to have changed their minds at the last minute and were consequently saved.

14

Our Curricular Needs and Social Rights

ALTHOUGH WE HAVE NOT HAD A CENSUS SINCE THE YEAR 1998, it is said that the population of Pakistan numbers four hundred million. Our primers and early textbooks show a mother cooking chappati on the griddle, the father smoking a hookah, the son playing, and the daughter helping her mother. Never is the girl shown playing or the mother resting. According to a recent survey by UNICEF, 25 million Pakistani children do not go to school. The reason for this is poverty, as well as illiteracy of the parents and their indifference to their children's education. In the villages one child among six or seven in a family is admitted to a madrasa. Another is sent to a mosque to memorize the Quran. A third son is sent to a motor workshop so he can learn the work, and a fourth is found a job in a tea stall. All these children earn a daily wage of about 10 to 20 rupees a day, which they hand over to their mother. This system has never changed in Pakistan. The UNICEF report also states that 50% of the children who are admitted to schools run away from school. There are two reasons for this: one is teachers do not have an interest in teaching and beat the children; two is that the lessons in the textbooks are not interesting and offer little variety since the themes are the same or similar in all the subjects.

In the 1940s, exhausted by World War ll, the British were eager to leave India. Under the Hindu-Muslim agreement, the area between Firozpur and Amritsar was given to the Hindus, and East Bengal, on account of its Muslim majority, became part of Pakistan. With a distance of a thousand miles between the two wings, the students of East and West Pakistan were not able to come close to one another. The physical distance turned into animosity, and in 1971 the new state of Bangladesh came into being. This huge political tremor did not leave much of a mark on the curriculum—just a line was introduced that said, 'East Pakistan has now separated and become Bangladesh.'

The curriculum should prescribe that one textbook in every class should have an interesting lesson on Quaid-e-Azam with a reference to his 11th August speech. Moreover, children should also be taught to respect all religions and not just their own, have peaceful and friendly links with other countries, exchange cultural and educational delegations with neighbouring countries. Their parents and teachers should teach them not to internalize biases. Dialogues in the form of graphic stories between Pakistan and a neighbouring country should be available for children to read.

Reading the Quran is not mandatory for non-Muslims. The curriculum should include descriptions of the religious festivals of other faiths, such as, Hinduism, Christianity, Zoroastrianism. After watching Indian movies our children are known to ask their parents, 'This was hardly a wedding; there were no *pheras*!' Everyday language also shows some the influence of Indian movies as many children like to call their parents Mataji and Pitaji. The television of each country has left its impact on the neighbouring country. When Mussarrat Nazir's wedding songs were at the height of their popularity and different rituals of *mehndi* and *mayoon* were shown in Bajia's television dramas, these ceremonies and their customs were imitated on the other side of the border. Pakistan too has not been immune to such influences.

Other than teaching, the curriculum schools have little to offer children. The typical village school does not even have a boundary wall around it. Most such schools have neither a bathroom nor any arrangement for drinking water. Even in urban areas it is not uncommon to see children carrying a water bottle to school. In the last few years computers have been given to schoolchildren. However, neither the children nor their teachers have the requisite proficiency in English to utilize this facility to its optimum. Instead they spend their time watching cartoon films or playing games on their computers.

The Punjab government and some NGOs have arranged evening classes for children who are employed in workshops. However, at the end of the working day these children are so exhausted that they take little interest in the education offered to them. They should have a curriculum based on the work they are doing in order to improve their efficiency at their work.

Efforts are being made to ensure that the number of children per family does not exceed three or four. In areas like Tharparkar infant mortality is very high owing to premature births and low birth weights. These areas do have maternity centres, but if there is the slightest complication in the delivery, the centre cannot deal with it. Consequently, the pregnant woman is taken to hospital on whatever ramshackle conveyance that happens to be available and driven to hospital over rough, bumpy roads. It is common for the child to be dead by the end of the ride, and sometimes even the mother does not survive.

The school curriculum should include teaching of first aid, traffic rules, and hygiene among other things. The classroom should provide hands-on training in these subjects. Sportsmanship and good manners should be taught on the school playground. It is a pity though that many or most of our schools have no playground. Legally no child under the age of 16 can be employed in a factory, and a labourer has to be paid the minimum wage of 12 thousand rupees per month. Again, by law, anyone who works more than eight hours a day has to be paid overtime. Yet countless parents willingly send their young children off to work in restaurants. Girls and boys employed by factories to sew clothes are told, 'No matter how long it takes to complete your work, if you leave before you've finished it, you will not be paid the full amount.'

Most of our schools do not have libraries. If your children go to such a school, buy them inexpensive books, encourage them to read, and also read out to them and let them read to you. This will give them confidence and improve their pronunciation. Do this at least once a month.

If you have a servant, give him the food that you eat and do not fob him off with the leftovers. If you do this, he will not steal from you.

Children, do buy a book every month. Tell your parents you would rather have a book than buy ice cream. Get your friends to do the same. Take a map of Pakistan and mark on it the places you dream of visiting. Then, save some money yourself and ask your parents for some. With the money you collect, go and see the places you have marked on the map, and then write about your travels and read out your account to your class. If you have a tablet or a cheap mobile phone, do not take it to school with you, and do not write and circulate abuses or other dirty stuff on it. If you do, you could be charged with cybercrime.

In village state schools, it is common practice to beat children with a rod. School violence of this kind is now coming into the open because children and their parents have begun to voice their grievance. Most of the time, the offending schoolteacher is let off with an admonishment. In the West if a child is abused by his teacher or parents, he can phone for the police.

There is a clause about right of divorce in the *nikahnama*, or marriage agreement. It is usually ignored by the bride's family, because to fill this column is considered a bad omen. If a husband and wife quarrel and issues like divorce and child support loom up, the matter goes to court. The right to divorce or *khula* for the woman asserted in the *nikahnama* at the beginning of the marriage would have made the procedure simpler as she could herself apply to the court for divorce.

Not just the big landowners and super rich but also common citizens can own a gun, as long as they have the requisite firearm licence, although they are not allowed to brandish it or use it without a cause that justifies using a weapon. However, in Pakistan it is customary to fire guns in celebration of a wedding or a victory at the polls. Accidents occur, and many people lose their lives as a consequence of the illegal shooting.

Brickmakers are a traditional part of labour in Pakistan. The children of brickmakers start to make bricks at a young age. The Punjab government has recently ordered that the children of brickmakers be educated and given a monthly sum of Rs. 1000.

To have one's own religion and adhere to it is a fundamental human right. It goes against fundamental rights to try to change someone's religion. Every individual has the right to practise his religion, celebrate religious festivals, and live in freedom.

Children are still tied up with chains in different parts of the country. Police or fundamental rights organizations try to free these children. Man was born free, and freedom is his basic right. But some actions do not fall under fundamental rights, for example writing obscene material on facebook, computers or the internet, and watching lewd movies on the computer. Parents and teachers can take measures against such activities. There is now also a law to punish them.

Animals too are entitled to fundamental rights. If they are kept as domestic animals or pets they have the right to be looked after, be inoculated against disease, given the right food, etc.

It is essential to knock before you enter a house or somebody's room. If there is no response to your knocking, you must leave the place. Every human being has the right to manage his personal matters. This too is a fundamental right.

Disabled children have fundamental rights too. In their homes, they should be given appropriate food and equal status with the other children in the house. When they are of school-going age, they should be sent to a special school. Nowadays disabled children are seated next to healthy children in the classroom, so that they are given the same education and learn to respect each other. However, dumb, deaf, and blind children are sent to special schools. In our villages such children are not given the kind of attention that is due to them. The government and NGOs have the responsibility of making arrangements for their education, and teaching other children to treat them in a friendly manner.

It is the duty of the local government to provide crossings where the disabled can cross busy roads. As in other countries special arrangements should be in place for the disabled in big buildings, in every shopping mall, cinema, and park. Today, many courageous blind young women and men who have learned to read and write with the help of Braille, are working for the Foreign Office, the United Nations and teaching in colleges.

The relationship between a husband and a wife is being discussed in the end simply because in some households, the husband starts beating the wife for the slightest offence. If the curry has not been heated to his satisfaction, he smashes her face with the dish. Having taken alcohol or drugs, if he comes home in the middle of the night or later, and the wife dares to ask him why he is so late, he will hit her with a rod, very often right in front of the children. Teachers and elders in the family should tell him that, in the first place, hitting someone for no reason is inhuman. Besides, indulging in such deeds in front of children leaves them devoid of all respect for their father. As they grow older they too develop a bad temper and treat their siblings and friends as they have seen their father treat their mother.

Many children are left-handed and their parents beat them, forcing them to write with their right hand. This attitude can destroy a child psychologically. Many children are drawn to art, poetry or writing prose. All such children should be encouraged to use their talent.

15

What Do Schools and Parents Teach Children

A T THE TIME OF PARTITION, THE SCHOOLS ESTABLISHED BY
the British were of two kinds. One kind of school had all
Christian teachers. A female Hindu Pandit taught Hindi and
a Muslim taught Urdu. These schools were part of the urban
environment. In rural areas there were fewer schools and more
madrasas. The Quran, philosophy, and *tib* or ancient Greek
medicine were taught in the madrasas; the latter two improved
under Muslim Arabs. Many rich Muslims and Hindus gave
donations to open schools where basic English was taught
in addition to Urdu and Hindi. English schools were private
schools. Children studied the Quran and learnt Urdu and Hindi
at home. In English schools they learnt and practised English
handwriting. At the age of five they sat for a test which qualified
them for admission in Class 1. Usually boys and girls who passed
their matric exam sat for the CT exam. Successful examinees
could then find jobs as primary school teachers. Those who
did their BA and then passed the BT exam became high school
teachers. This tradition has continued to this day in government
schools. Private schools and especially private nursery schools
came into fashion in the Ayub Khan era. The reason was that
not all children could be accommodated in the state schools.

Another reason was that teachers retiring from English schools had started opening private primary schools of their own. In these schools children did not have to sit on mats. Chairs were provided for them and the schools charged high fees. Students of these schools could bring their own water and lunch boxes, while state school children bought snacks like chickpeas and *chaat* from vendors standing outside their school.

While the number of state schools grew, population and with it the private schools proliferated. The government did nothing to prevent the spread of private schools. The teachers started another business of giving private tuitions. The students who came to them for tuition were not necessarily weak in their studies. Among them were those who hoped to improve their grades by taking tuition from their class teacher. More than half the well-heeled parents who were too lazy to teach their children, sent them to tutors. Children's education became confined to textbooks. School libraries did not lend books to students fearing that they would damage or lose them. Few parents thought that reading books and borrowing them from libraries was important for their children. Also, few parents cared to send their children to radio stations to take part in radio programmes.

The joint family system was breaking down. Educated parents were looking for separate homes for their nuclear families, because they did not want to leave their children with their grandparents. Consequently, the custom of nightly storytelling for the young by the older generation came to an end. Nowadays children are put to bed where they can go to sleep watching television programmes. Tiny tots are left before the television set with milk bottles in their hands, their mouths gripping the nipple and their eyes stuck to the screen, transfixed by the cartoon they are watching.

From watching cartoons the child graduates to using the cell phone. The subsequent immersion in the Facebook world is self-propelled and self-taught, and by then books become superfluous to him. Prestigious English schools teach more of foreign classics and very little Urdu literature or Pakistan's history. Most students of prestigious private English schools leave the country after their A Levels to pursue their education abroad. Meanwhile, students of state schools become clerks or contractors. Their parents or wives are delighted when they go home with a little money in their pockets. Nowadays their children demand chocolates but never books.

School curriculums do not offer human rights, fundamental rights, the rights of children or the rights of citizens. Nor are the children ever taught these subjects. Neither parents nor teachers give thought to the problems of growing children. Rudderless generations grow up and are absorbed in little but unrestrained propagation.

Since the last few years, students of private schools are being taught new lessons on the computer. Examination questions and answers are also typed on the computer screen. Interviews are conducted on Skype. But despite all this, the importance of voting and the need and importance of identity cards are never taught or explained. Married couples involved in the tensions of the matrimonial state are busy procreating. Neither had studied the details of the marriage contract, nor had their parents. They simply accepted whatever was filled in by the marriage registrar in accordance with the tradition and his own lights. Later if the marriage turned sour and issues of divorce or child support were faced, the husband and wife were compelled to frequent family courts. There is little chance of compromise.

Students who train in technical schools usually look for jobs in other countries, attracted by the higher salaries offered there. For the sake of dollars, pounds, euros, riyals and dirhams, as many as four labourers willingly share a single room, save their money, and send it home. Aspiring to educate their children and own lavish homes, these hard working men also try to have their grown children take over their jobs when they retire thereby spreading the trend for disorganized families and disrupted family life.

Doctors and engineers prefer not to start their career by working in rural areas. Jobs in these areas do not provide them with a place to live, nor are medicines and the necessary tools supplied to them there, despite the fact that on paper all of this has been made available to them.

All these problems have not prevented the emergence of some highly gifted children. Arfa Karim made such a name as a computer expert that Bill Gates expressed a desire to meet her. She died at the age of sixteen. Malala Yusufzai of Swat was shot by terrorists, but despite her horrible experience, she continued her studies and as the Nobel Laureate for peace has propagated the importance of spreading education. Many young boys made their names in fields as diverse as Snooker and Computers.

In 1979, Dr Abdus Salaam, a Pakistani, was given the Nobel Prize in Physics. Many brave young men defended Pakistan and were given the Nishan-e-Haider. Benazir Bhutto was twice made the Prime Minister. Each time, she was the only woman in the Islamic world to occupy this office.

Today Pakistani scientists, doctors, and artists are famous throughout the world. Paintings by Shazia Sikandar and Imran Quraishi are priced at hundreds of thousands of dollars. In Karachi, Dr Adeeb Rizvi is doing memorable work by saving the lives of countless patients without charging them anything. Similarly, the Shaukat Khanum Memorial Hospital treats many thousands of cancer patients. The Mary Adelaide Leprosy Centre in Karachi treats and keeps leprosy patients who are not welcome even in their homes. Volunteering in this centre are mostly Parsee and Christian women.

Parents should tell their children about all of this in the form of stories. They should also tell them what the country was like when their own parents migrated or lived here. Electricity was not available almost anywhere, as it is now, so kerosene lanterns and petro-maxes were commonly used. In the absence of electric fans, large cloth fans hanging from the ceiling were pulled with ropes attached to them, their ends wound round the thumb of the puller. Ice cream was made at home in a manually worked machine. Our parents were not rich, and not ashamed of wearing patched clothes. They worked hard to give us a better future. A reminder of those days is the cobbler who sits under a tree by the roadside, sewing soles to worn shoes in order to disguise the poverty of the wearer.

16

Our Houses: New and Old

AFTER PARTITION, GOVERNMENT SERVANTS WHO HAD BEEN brought to Karachi in special trains were accommodated in quarters vacated by the British. Parsees, Memons, Bohris, Christians, and Hindus rarely migrated to India from Karachi. However, from all the rest of West Pakistan, Hindus migrated to India, while a large number of Muslims, from Deccan and Bihar to Amritsar, moved to Pakistan. Houses vacated by Hindus in Pakistan were mostly double-storied. Houses evacuated in India were usually single-storied. The department dealing with allotments allotted one storey to one family and the second storey to another family. Electricity was available in Lahore and other cities in Pakistan, like Faisalabad, Karachi, Hyderabad, and Multan.

In the olden days houses had a courtyard, a verandah, and a *dubari*. The *dubari* was the part of the house where the water carrier would bring the water and cry 'Ladies, go behind the curtain I am going to fill your water vessels.' The courtyard was where relatives and other guests were seated when they visited. They were offered beetle leaf (*paan*), cardamom, and nothing else. Tea and food was offered only to those who had been invited to a meal celebrating a birthday or an *aqiqa*. Parties in those days were very different from parties today.

In summer inmates of a house slept in the courtyard. If it rained during the night, the charpoys were pulled into the verandah. The kitchen was in one corner of the courtyard. In another corner sacks filled with grain were stored. Four or five years after the birth of Pakistan, latrines dug into the floor on the roofs of houses were eliminated. These latrines used to be built inside small bathrooms and were cleaned by a sweeper woman. Servants were not employed for housework. Women and girls in every house cooked the food, washed the dishes and did the laundry.

Karachi is the largest city in Pakistan in terms of population and industry. In the 1980s Afghan settlements began to emerge here. Nowadays most of Karachi's transport is in the hands of Pathans. The city is dotted with apartment buildings of four, five, and more storeys. Nevertheless in every corner of the city there are squatter settlements populated by poor people from southern Punjab and interior Sind. The Steel Mill and Port Qasim have their own colonies. Nowadays offices of private companies, flats, farmhouses, and the largest mosque in Pakistan are being built along the road from Karachi to Hyderabad. However, there is little interest in building a cultural centre or auditorium.

Most men in the past, especially those hailing from Lahore's inner city, used to work for the railways. They used to leave their homes for the Mughalpura Railway Workshop at 6 a.m., their lunch boxes dangling from the handle bars of their bicycles. Since three families were accommodated in every house, home for each family was just one room. There was a common kitchen with separate stoves. Even now, in mud coated yards of houses in the villages, there are two or three separately placed stoves. Earlier there used to be hand pumps in the market square. Men would fill buckets with water from the pumps and bring them home where women stored it in tanks and mud vessels. In rural areas such as from Balochistan to southern Punjab and Tharparkar, the government sets up a hand pump in the centre of the village even now, which provides water to all the people of the area. Men take their bath under the water pump.

Earlier there used to be a single light bulb in a house placed where children could read and write by its light. However, even today a village house is lighted by a single bulb. Studying under street lamps, children from relatively poor houses of the city not only passed their exams but also achieved officers' posts. All the cities now have electricity but the electric supply is often irregular. From Lahore to northern Punjab, industry and population have grown. However, cultural awareness has not kept pace, though interest in food has intensified.

Since Balochistan receives little rain, many houses are built with mud walls. However, climate change has increased the chances of rain. Many houses are now made with cement blocks. Houses in Punjab and Sind have courtyards, but there are no courtyards in Balochistan because in winter most areas get snowfall, while in summer places like Sibbi are intensely hot. In the olden days the floor of a whole room in a Baloch house was spread with a carpet. In winter, the entire family would sleep on that carpet. However, in the last 20 years, television has effected a change in that. Beds, sofas and some other furniture can now be seen in Baloch homes. Hand pumps for drawing water have been erected in most areas, more by NGOs and fewer by the government. Bigger houses have water tanks. People now have also built toilets with the squat commode in their houses.

Houses of Khans are like palaces, where servants are given food as well as old, cast off clothes. Salaries are unknown. In addition to doing the housework, servants' womenfolk are expected to embellish garments for the ladies of the house with Baloch embroidery. Buildings in areas such as Fort Sandeman and Zhob, where the British had their cantonment are used as residences for senior officers.

From the time of the British, water was collected in Balochistan and supplied to fields and orchards through *karezes*. A favourite pastime of young men was to sit by these and eat mangoes after cooling them in the water.

Doors and windows of carved wood are made in Khyber Pakhtunkhwa and are famous all over the world. Carved wooden doors are sold in Swat. In Khyber Pakhtunkhwa, even if a building is modern it usually has carved doors and windows in the old style. The Mahabat Khan Mosque in Peshawar is very famous.

At the time of Partition few women used to step out of their houses. However, after Quaid-e-Azam said that women must walk shoulder to shoulder with men, many women began to drape themselves with chadors and go to schools and colleges.

Begum Zari Sarfaraz, Begum Mehmooda Saleem, and Maryam Bibi have worked for social uplift all their lives. Like Punjab, the houses in KPK have courtyards. However, unlike Punjab the toilet is not on the roof but in a corner of the courtyard. The squat commode was present from British days. Abbotabad had an army cantonment like Peshawar, so houses started to be built with cement from 1905. After the discovery of Takht Bahi, hotels were built in Naushehra to accommodate tourists. In Kohat and Kerk, there is a custom of forced marriages for girls. In Swabi and Hazara old houses are being demolished and new ones constructed in their place. Some new houses were built because countless houses were destroyed in 2005 due to earthquake. The whole of Mansehra was devastated by the earthquake. There too most people built their houses all over again. In Balakot too, the houses that were built the second time were constructed in the new style.

In Azad Kashmir the area stretching from Muzafferabad to Bagh was badly affected by the 2005 earthquake, and all the houses in the region were razed. Help came in many forms from local and international institutions. Turkey reconstructed a girls' college in Muzafferabad and the Secretariat. Many local NGOs began to work hard right after the earthquake. NGOs, like the NRSP rebuilt mainly Bagh and its adjoining areas. Since this area receives snowfall, the houses there have sloping roofs as in Britain, protected by tin sheets. But many houses are also built with wood because wood that comes from this area is long-lasting and inexpensive.

Kalash and Chitral also receive a lot of snowfall. All the houses there are made of wood, and many houses are approached by climbing steps. The Kalashi women make bead necklaces, and sew the special Kalashi garments and caps worn by the people in the region. There did not use to be any mosques in Kalash, however, now there are several.

Bahawalpur used to be a princely state in India, and then in Pakistan, but in 1955 it was merged with Pakistan (then, West Pakistan). The ruler of the state had seven palaces, including Noor Mehel and Darbar Mehel. At 18 kilometres from Bahawalpur district is Khanqah Sharif, which is the shrine of Khawaja Mohkumud Deen Serani. Close to Bahawalpur is the Cholistan desert where a large area is dotted with farmhouses. The people here are poor, and like the people of Tharparkar they get their drinking water from small manmade ponds called *tobas*.

Like Lahore, the city of Bahawalpur has several gates. The houses are old and the streets narrow. And yet, as in city centre Lahore, young men can be seen riding their motor bikes everywhere. The language of Bahawalpur is similar to Siraiki. New settlements are proliferating. Many people build arches in their houses which resemble arches in the palaces. With the establishment of a university in Bahawalpur, girls and boys from other areas come here for their education and take admission in the institution. Like the Bahawalpur University, Sargoda, Gujrat, and Multan Universities are opening campuses even in Lahore and Sialkot.

Islamabad is the city of privilege. It is a modern city with some old establishments such as Golra Sharif and Bari Imam's shrine where every year the *urs* is held. With a red stole over them, people beat drums, and throngs of devotees arrive for the *urs*. All the villages around Islamabad have gradually transformed into urban areas. Many flats are being built for the rich. Meanwhile the poor or lower middle class survive on promises. Islamabad and Rawalpindi are known as twin cities. The population of both cities has grown to the extent that even though each has its own Municipal Committee, the distance between the two cities is almost non-existent. Islamabad has spread up till Taxila, and Wah has grown to join Hasanabdal. More examples of such convergences are Murree entering the boundaries of Rawalpindi, and Nathiagali in KPK. One can reach Abbottabad through Baragali and Kalabagh. Old houses in Abbottabad are being converted into hotels.

In Sind, in places which had army cantonments, like Khairpur, there used to be large houses with wide courtyards, verandahs, storerooms, and several large rooms. In Sukkhar and Hyderabad single storey houses had ventilators on their roofs, for in these places, like Karachi, a cool breeze blows in the evening which can cool the whole house. After Partition when the population began to grow, multi-storey houses, and staff quarters and flats were built for government employees. The numbers of such residential units has been growing. These days, multi-purpose buildings are being constructed with restaurants, cinemas and grocery centres.

The tradition of pirs or religious leaders and their disciples is widespread. Not only is the annual *urs* held at the shrines of Shah Abdul Latif Bhitai and Sachal Sarmast attended by throngs of devotees, even on ordinary days there are crowds of enthusiastic adherents. In 1974 the states of Khairpur, Hunza, Swat, and Kalat were merged into the appropriate provinces.

In the Gilgit and Skardu division, which includes Hunza, Nagar, and Khaplu, there is a lot of snowfall, so houses are made out of wood. Many nomadic tribes go down to warmer lands along with their herds of cattle. Those who stay back eat food that they have prepared for the severe winter, such as dried meat and also plenty of dried vegetables. Gilgit Baltistan is politically a province and even has a regular assembly, a governor, and a chief minister so is Azad Kashmir. It has been given autonomy and has the administrative powers of a province.

Now, the old British law that governs FATA is going to end and the Pakistani law is to be implemented very shortly. All of this area is mountainous. People make their homes in the mountains, but some regular houses have also been constructed. Many hundreds of thousands of people who were made homeless during the army action of Zarb-e-Azb now live in tents. Because Waziristan is not altogether free of terrorists, some NGOs have established health centres and one room schools for the tent dwellers. Despite the severe heat of summer and the harsh cold of winter, the people here are forced to live in their tents. However, IDPs are returning to their homes which will be completed in 2017.

17

Our National Languages

BASICALLY URDU IS OUR NATIONAL LANGUAGE AND MEDIUM of communication. Each language spoken in our country mutates after about 10 miles or so. These changes are sometimes in intonation, sometimes in pronunciation and sometimes in meaning. In Punjab, the Punjabi language spoken from Lahore to Jehlum is more or less the same. But changes are apparent if one goes to Sargodha or Chakwal. Women there call a shirt '*chakka*' and *ghio* '*keo*'. Similarly, a little further, between Gojar Khan and Attock the intonation is that of Potohari Punjabi. As we advance from there we hear more and more of the Pashto language. Afghan immigrants who have been living in KPK and Balochistan for 30 years are able to understand Darri, the language spoken by 30 lakh people living in that area. People living on the hundreds of miles long KPK and Balochistan border speak Balochi, Darri, Brahwi, and Punjabi, in addition to Pashto.

There are three categories of people in Balochistan—those who speak Brahvi, those who speak Pashto, and those who speak Balochi. The Punjabis who settled in some areas of Balochistan after the 1935 earthquake speak all these languages in addition to Punjabi. Moreover, people from all parts of Balochistan, whether it is Pasni or Gwadar, and whether they are fishermen, or people of some other persuasion, can all understand and even speak Urdu. The main reason for this is that even before Partition, Urdu was the common language of communication.

In Sind people everywhere speak Sindi, Urdu, Pashto, as well as Punjabi. The reason is that much of the transport and other buisnesses are in the hands of Pathans, Punjabis, and Afghans. Sindhi is used in offices as well as taught in schools. Urdu is not only taught in educational institutions, it is also the mother language of people who migrated to Pakistan during Partition. The Riyasati language, a combination of Siraiki, Sindhi, and Punjabi is spoken around Rahimyar Khan. From Multan to Bahawalpur and DG Khan pure Siraiki is spoken. Its intonation and vocabulary are different, but it is a sweet language. Because Urdu is part of the curriculum from grade 1, everyone from adults to children and speak it. Nowadays poetry and short stories are published in Siraiki and magazines are brought out in the language.

In Gilgit Baltistan people speak Balti among themselves. Sheena, Wafi, Burushaski, Khawar, and Domki are also languages of Gilgit Baltistan but they are rarely written. In offices people write in either Urdu or English like in the rest of Pakistan. Gilgit-Baltistan are two divisions, and Shigar, Ghanchai and Kharmung are among their districts. Several languages are spoken by the people but they are not written. Even if they are written the script used is Urdu. Burushaski is spoken in Gujal and Khunjrab. In villages closer to Kashmir, the language spoken in Dogri.

Here begins the territory of the Kashmiri language. Kashmiri is spoken from Jammu to Muzafferabad. Some people speak Dogri and Gojri. Urdu is taught in schools and colleges. In areas such as Mirpur and Rawlakot, the language spoken is Punjabi. It should be remembered that Maulana Mohammad Husain Azad and Maulana Hali worked hard for the development of Urdu in Punjab. They were urged by the British to do so.

In the days of the Moghuls, Persian was spoken and used for official communication. Currently English is gaining importance in state and private schools, and colleges. In the media although there are channels for every language, English is mixed up in each language. In the Moghul era Persian was the official language besides being the spoken language for many. With the British, the use of English rose in the subcontinent. Today it is used in schools and colleges as well as the media. Even local languages are plentifully peppered with English.

Gujrati and Sindhi languages have their own newspapers. Urdu newspapers are published in every province. English newspapers are published from all the provincial capitals as well as the national capital. One Urdu newspaper can be bought for Rs. 2 and is read by shopkeepers. Husain Naqvi had brought out a Punjabi newspaper but it was shut down under Zia ul-Haq. Shah Mohammad Murri brings out the monthly *Sanggat*, in Urdu and Balochi.

18
Our Vegetation

THERE IS MUCH REFERENCE TO THE FLOWER AND THE nightingale in our poetry and literature. So let us meet some of them.

In summers when even the grass is scorched, flowers such as the *motia*, the *raat ki rani* and the *sada bahar* spread their fragrance from earthen pot placed in courtyards. Pakistan has 430 species of trees and 830 of flowers. There are also 236 flowering plants that are grown from grafts even in other countries outside Pakistan. Many flowering plants are grown from seedlings and later repotted in pots or in flowerbeds. In the middle of summer or end winter many kinds of marigolds flower. The marigold plays an important role in all Hindu rites and celebrations. In Pakistan, strings of marigold are used to decorate stages in functions.

There are 2000 types of roses in the world. Pattoki is a city in the Kasur district of Punjab, famous for its flowers and especially for roses. From November to March the Pattoki district grows the most roses, followed by Kalarkahar, Jahangira, and Nizam, where roses are grown over many acres of land. Nainsukh is the market where roses are bid for and eventually arrive in the different cities of Pakistan. In November and December one sees the chrysanthemum everywhere. Its stalk is thin and the flower is heavy, so the stalks and branches have to be supported.

Like the marigold some flowers have religious significance. The presence of a basil plant is mandatory in temples. The champak flowers are seen in summer. The *din ka raja* (literally, ruler of the day) is not very fragrant. It blooms during the day and closes its petals at night. For a few weeks in the hot, rainy summer the lazy daisy, cockscomb, and snapdragon, show their vibrant colours. Sunflowers can be seen spread over acres of land in the province of Sind. In the Matiari area the *motia* has a lavish flowering. Among perennial creepers the *har singhar*, bougainvillea, and supra creeper come from Karachi, Lahore and Tila Gung. For six weeks you can see the flowers and buds of *amaltas, kachnar, gulcheen*, and *gul chandni*. The *chambeli* or jasmine is the national flower of Pakistan. It is a delicate flower and is seen in spring. In the hot summers, zinnias, pansies, latanas and marigolds can be seen. At the end of the rainy season, the narcissus, placed in a vase at home give out their fragrance for a week.

Some flowers used to be imported, but now they are grown locally. Among them is the tuberose, the gladiola, and the chrysanthemum. These flowers are now grown in Swat, Karachi, and many other cities. The cactus grows in all of Tharparkar, Cholistan, and all other such sandy areas. It can be planted and also grows spontaneously.

The Japanese art form of bonsai, or growing miniature trees in containers or pots is now also practised in Pakistan. The trees are never taller than 1.5 foot, and are very expensive to buy.

The land in Pakistan is very fertile. Every area has its own local flowers, fruits, plants, and trees. From the Potohar region to Afghanistan the poppy grows spontaneously. The government has them destroyed but the land throws them up again. The poppy is used to make narcotics, which are smuggled abroad causing many people to be arrested and giving the country a bad name.

19

Pakistani Fruits

THE POET GHALIB HAD SAID THAT THE MANGO MUST HAVE two qualities: it must be sweet, and available in large quantities. However, in Ghalib's days a much smaller variety of mango was available, compared to now. With the month of April the fruit starts coming from Sind, and supply of various kinds of mango continues until September. First to come is the large, sweet Sindhri, followed by Fujri, Malda, and Sandori. As the summer temperatures rise the Chausa, Langra, and Tota pari arrive. The rainy season is the time for the splendid Anwar Ratole mango to emerge. With it comes the Tapka mango, sucked for its sweet juice. There was a time when people would buy these mangoes, collect them in a bucket and suck, sitting in Shalimar gardens.

There are several delicious recipes in which the mango stars. There is the *guramba,* which is made by mixing mango flesh with jaggery syrup. The unripe mango is used to make a cold drink and also chutney. Mango pickles are well known and very popular.

The banana used to be available only in summer but now it is obtainable throughout the year. Raw bananas are cooked like

154

vegetables. Bananas are also used in desserts, and considered harmless and even restorative if eaten when one has diarrhea.

There are many kinds of apples available in Pakistan. The apple from Kashmir is large and red. Apples come from Swat, Kohat, and Murree as well, but the apple from Balochistan is very tasty. There is one variety of apple known as the golden apple. It is sweet, juicy, and a little sour. People like it very much. There are now many varieties of the golden apple. Pakistan also imports apples from Iran. They are known as Mashadi apples after the city Mashad. These apples have a soft flesh and are therefore liked by children, old people, and the sick.

With the start of winter, piles of fruiter, a variety of orange, can be seen at fruitsellers'. This is an inexpensive fruit and everybody can afford to eat it. When it gets colder the varieties known as *malta* and *kino* arrive in the market. The red *malta* comes from Khanpur but is available at the end of winter. The grapefruit and *mosambi* join the other citrus fruit when winter is at its coldest. All these fruits are exported to Afghanistan and many other countries. *Malta* juice is popular throughout Pakistan.

The guava is grown in all seasons and many parts of Pakistan. Sometimes it comes from Kohat and sometimes from Larkana. Smaller areas produce many varieties of guava. In Larkana guavas are sometimes eaten with bread.

At the end of summer and beginning of winter the pear and its variety the *babugosha* are found plentifully especially in Murree. The *babugosha* is an extremely juicy fruit. Concurrently with the pear comes the peach. The first to arrive in the market are peaches from Swat and Murree. They are fat, golden, and juicy. Hotels sell peach and apricot juice. Apricots from Hunza and Gilgit are big and very sweet. Apricots are used to make a dessert which looks like custard. Apricots are sold fresh or dried. They are used in Sindhi biryani and also eaten on their own as a dried fruit.

Dates come in seven varieties. Some of them have no stone. The best dates in Pakistan come from Khairpur. Many people have dates with their breakfast to make up for lack of vitamins. The date has been mentioned in the Quran. The Prophet (PBUH) was very fond of this fruit. Breaking one's fast with a date is a sunnah.

Despite their conflicts, trade in fruit between KPK and Afghanistan never suffered. In summer especially, but also in other seasons, the *sarda* and *garma* are available in diferent lengths and thicknesses. Afghans do not bake bread at home. They buy their *naan* and often eat it with *garma* or *sarda* and green onions. Many Afghans, who have lived in Pakistan for 30 years or so, now eat their bread, Pakistani style, with curry.

There are many varieties of grapes and pomegranates. The Qandhari variety is very sweet. One kind of pomegranates, the seeds in which have less flesh and less juice is known locally as the *bedana* and is available everywhere.Qandhari pomegranates and grapes are widely available from August to October. The bigger variety of grape has seeds and is dried. The smaller, seedless varieties are also dried. *Sundarkhani* grapes are famous for their delicious taste.

In the rainy season and early winter the persimmon, custard apple, and green coconut are available in large quantities. Coconut water from the green coconut is popular with the people of Karachi. In early summer the lychee arrives, especially from KPK. Strawberries and cherries are grown in mountainous places like Hunza. They are sold packed in small boxes all over the country.

Early in summer the water melon arrives. A little later come the melon, *lokaat*, the small berry known as *falsa*, the *chikoo* or sapodilla; but just before these fruits arrive, the fruit of the jujub tree, or *baer*, is ubiquitously available. In local medicine the *baer* is given as much importance for its vitamins as is the fig. *Baer* and persimmon are considered poor man's fruits. The papaya grows easily in Karachi. Grown in this city it has a taste unequalled by papaya grown anywhere else except in Delhi.

Jamun berries cover trees in the rainy season. In summer the *qumrukh*, another poor people's fruit, is sold. It is sour, so people sprinkle it with salt before eating it. Not much of it is grown in Pakistan.

Dried fruit are traded between Afghanistan and Pakistan and are popularly eaten in the winter months. Walnuts, almonds, currants, are eaten by the rich. The poor settle for peanuts. Pine nuts are too expensive to be eaten by all.

20

Vegetables of Pakistan

IN PAKISTAN A PROFUSE VARIETY OF VEGETABLES IS GROWN AND eaten in every season. In winter seven or eight types of salad leaves and many varieties of spinach are available. Originally village fare, but now appreciated in affluent city households as well, the *sarsoon ka saag* and maize flour bread are very popular. Also in winter the white, red, and yellow turnips are a pleasing sight. Even before the arrival of winter the cauliflower and cabbage are seen in the markets. *Qulfa* is another kind of saag, different from spinach. Peas and green beans of different kinds fill the greengrocers' shops.

Pumpkins and gourds are summer vegetables. With *tori* or zucchini, okra, bitter gourd, local and larger *tindas*, come green onions, beetroot, *mongra*, *cholia*. For salads, lettuce, iceberg, and cucumber are available.

With the start of winter, *kachnar* or bauhinia trees are full of their fruit. Tomatoes are grown all the year round and are used in almost all curries. Onions too are used in practically all curries and also pickled in vinegar. Some people eat raw onions as salad. In some places *arvi* or arum leaves are eaten as well as the arum vegetable itself. Sweet potatoes are eaten boiled. They are also cooked with milk to be eaten as kheer. All curries use garlic and ginger. Lemon juice is used in cold drinks as well as in salads. Radishes are mostly eaten raw as salad. Sometimes they are cooked along with their leaves. Cauliflower and radishes are sometimes used (individually) as fillings for parathas. Peas are often cooked with rice as pea pulao. Capsicums come in green, yellow, and red colours. They are cooked in different ways. Brinjals can be either round or long. They are cooked as a sour and spicy curry on their own, with potatoes, or mashed in the form known as *bhurta*. Potatoes are available all the year round. They are used to make chips, and are also cooked with other vegetables or meat. Mushrooms are available only in small numbers. Usually they are grown on farms and are marketed in boxes. In a vegetable pulao, many kinds of vegetables are cooked with rice. Carrots are popular for their juice. They are also much in demand for making halwa and *gajrela*, and cooking with other vegetables.

21

Our Canal System, Electricity and Gas Reserves

PAKISTAN'S CANAL SYSTEM IS ONE OF THE GREAT CANAL
systems of the world. Planned by the British in the beginning
of the twentieth century, it is considered the best man-made
canal system in the world. At the time of Partition river water
was also divided, under an agreement. It is known as the Indus
Water Treaty. Before the last 30 years canal water was used only
for irrigation. The 3 mile long Sukkhar Barrage is the longest of
all the barrages built by the British. Its construction was started
in 1923. The headwork of this barrage was completed in 1932.
There are 1,360 canals in Sind. Collectively they are known
as the Nara Irrigation system. This system caters to Khairpur,
Sanghar, Mirpurkhas, and up to Jamrao Canal in Tharparkar.
The river Chenab has the Rasool headwork. The Qadirabad
Link Canal and the Balonki Link issue from it. Rohri Canal
has the Ghotki feeder. All these canals divide into smaller canals
and finally merge into the Indus River. River Indus is 3,180
km. long. It has many barrages among which are the Taunsa,
Sukkhar, Kotri, Guddoo and Chashma barrages. Currently there
are three big reservoirs in Pakistan. There are also six barrages,
and twelve inter link canals.

Altogether there are 57 long or short canals. Doabs formed by the Ravi river are the Upper and Lower Doabs. The Chhaj Doab is formed by the upper and lower Jehlum. From lower Jehlum the water goes past Sialkot and into the Chenab. Jhang gets its water from Jehlum and Chenab rivers. Haripur is fed by the Ghazi Barotha Canal. The Chashma Barrage yields hydroelectric power as well. The Begari Canal Bridge is in Jacobabad. The Tarbela Dam is on the River Indus as it flows through Khyber Pakhtunkhwa. The Shirki Dam is in Ghazi Barotha and Shirki. It is well known that the Tarbela Dam is the largest earth-filled dam in the world. The Mangla Dam is on the river Jehlum, and is situated in Kashmir near the town of Mirpur. It is one of the five largest dams in Pakistan. Its main function is to improve irrigation in the area, but it also generates electric power. Lower and Upper canals in Swat get water from the Kabul river. The Sirhind Canal starts from the Ropar headworks. The Warsak Dam is built in the Kabul River close to Peshawar.

The Kachhi Canal is in Balochistan. Presently, subterranean watercourses provide most of the water for irrigation and drinking. Most of the large barrages in Pakistan are in Khyber Pakhtunkhwa, Sind, and Punjab. In Balochistan there are thirty dams of various sizes. Hub Dam is the largest among them.

These barrages provide water through 52 km long canals. About 100 small dams are under construction in Balochistan. The Hub Dam situated on the Sind-Balochistan border is the third largest dam in Pakistan. It provides water mainly to Karachi. The Mirani Dam is under construction on the Dasht River. The Gomal Zam Dam is in South Waziristan. The Ghazi Barotha

Dam on the Indus is located in Attock, in the province of Punjab. It also provides 1450 MW of electricity.

In Balochistan, the irrigation works of the Subkzai are under construction. A large part of Khyber Pakhtunkhwa receives its water and electricity through the Tarbela Dam. The Chashma Barrage provides water to Dera Ismail Khan. The issue of the Kalabagh Dam is still under discussion. At present there are many dams still under construction in KP. The Waran Canal was opened in 2015. It is part of the Gomalzam Dam project. The Gomal Dam is made of concrete and was made with the participation of WAPDA, in FATA. In Azad Kashmir a new dam is being built at the confluence of the Neelum and Jehlum rivers. It will provide electricity to most of Azad Kashmir.

The last two or three years have seen the emergence of solar energy in Pakistan. A few homeowners have already installed the system in their homes for their electricity needs. In many large cities traffic signals are run on the solar system. At Jhimpir, Sind, a 50 MG wind power project has been installed. Windmills have also been installed between Karachi and Hyderabad. Contacts have been made with friendly countries for creating electric power through nuclear energy. Agreements have also been made with friendly countries for the supply of gas, since Pakistan's need for this resource has grown with the rise in population and the expansion of cities.

The supply of water from canals having become inadequate, it is expected that the new dams will make up for the deficiency. As for gas, it was first discovered in Sui, a sub district of Dera

Bugti, in the year 1952, and named after the area of its origin. Gas and oil were also found in Kandhkot, Adhi, Mazarani, Chachar, Hala, and Gumbat. Sui Gas began to be supplied to houses in big cities in the year 1955.

However, a piped gas supply is still not available in all of Balochistan. In these areas gas is supplied in cylinders to homes and hotels. In at least 30% of Pakistani homes there is no gas supply. So, people are obliged to cook their food using dried twigs, dung cakes, or wood for fuel.

Until 20 years ago in the area from Kashmir to Punjab, it was customary for people to keep themselves warm in the harsh winters with the help of a *kangri*, a fire pot with live coals. Women would hold it under their chador and stay warm in their houses. Men in those cold climates would gather to sit around a fire and chat. However, now in most households, families sit together to watch television.

22

Our English Novelists and Poets

THE FIRST PAKISTANI WRITER TO PRODUCE A NOVEL IN English was Ahmed Ali. His work *Twilight in Delhi* was much acclaimed even beyond the frontiers of Pakistan. Taufiq Rafat and Daud Kamal were early writers of English poetry in Pakistan. Maki Kureishi and Zebunnissa Hamidullah were early female poets writing in English. The poet Kaleem Omar was a journalist as well as a poet. N.M. Rashid's son Shehryar Rashid who worked for the Ministry of Foreign Affairs and was Pakistan's ambassador in Uzbekistan wrote poetry in English. A collection of his poetry was published after his death from a heart attack.

Bapsi Sidhwa first became known for her novel *The Crow Eaters*. Her first novel was *The Bride*. The Parsi community was offended by it on account of its description of how the Zoroastrian religion treats women. However, the novel made Sidhwa famous in Pakistan and abroad. In the US where she later went and taught in a university, she wrote two novels: *An American Brat* and *Ice Candy Man*. About the same time her first novel *The Bride* was republished. The story of this novel revolves round a girl who, afraid at the prospect of a forced marriage, runs away from home but falls into the hands of

Pathans. She manages to run away a second time but undergoes much suffering and dies. *Zaitoon* is the name of this novel's Urdu translation.

Tehmina Durrani wrote on the life of Abdus Sattar Edhi. She became famous with her book *My Feudal Lord* which recounted the life she spent with her first husband, Mustafa Khar. The book shows what hypocritical lives the rich landlords of Pakistan live, and how poorly they treat their women. Tehmina's book was translated into many languages. It is a book you will find among those placed alongside *I am Malala* in airport bookshops. Malala Yusufzai's book, co-written with Christina Lamb is her memoir. It has sold thousands of copies. Many people have criticized it, but that has not affected the sales of the book.

The first novel by Mohammad Hanif, a young journalist-cum-fiction writer had for its centerpiece the death of the military dictator General Zia ul-Haq. The book, *A Case of Exploding Mangoes*, won awards and made its writer famous. Mohsin Hamid is the much acclaimed writer of novels like *Moth Smoke,* and *The Reluctant Fundamentalist,* which has been made into an award winning film. Kamila Shamsie has written several novels, among which is *Burnt Shadows*, a work that has been widely translated and was shortlisted for the Orange Prize. Her mother Muniza Shamsie is a senior journalist as well as a writer. Amir Husain has written short stories. Two collections of Danial Muinuddin's short stories have been published, and translated into many languages. They focus on south Punjab. H.M. Naqvi was born in London in the year 1973. He wrote a novel titled *Home Boy.*

The Shadow of the Crescent Moon is the first novel of Fatima Bhutto a scion of the famous and tragic Bhutto family. It is set in Mir Ali, a small town in Pakistan's tribal area. Its action takes place in the course of one morning. Nadeem Aslam's family was forced to flee Pakistan during the rule of General Zia ul-Haq on account of his father's Communist affinities. He has written several fine novels including *The Blind Man's Garden*, and *Maps for Lost Lovers*. His novels have won many awards, and he is a Fellow of the Royal Society of Literature.

Tariq Ali, a writer and broadcaster based in the UK, is a socialist. His book *The Duel* is about the history of Pakistan. He has written several other books some of which are novels centering on Islamic history.

Ibad Akhter wrote about Muslims in the US in his book *American Dervish*. Nafeesa Haji is the author of the novel *The Writing on my Forehead*. Rafia Zakaria wrote a novel about a woman's memories of Karachi. Tariq Fatah painted a picture of the longstanding hatred between Jews and Muslim.

Poetry

Alamgir Hashmi, Adrian Husain and Ehsan Sehgal have written good poetry in English. *High Noon and the Body*, a collection of poetry by Kaila Pasha is worthy of attention.

Translations

Mohammad Umar Memon and C.M. Naim have translated

novels and poetry by Intezar Husain, Khalida Husain, Deputy Nazir Ahmed, and myself. Shehnaz Faqiruddin has done a beautiful translation of *Tilism-e-Hoshruba*. Asif Farrukhi and Rakhshanda Jalil also have translated the works of Intezar Husain and this writer.

23

Our Provinces and Regions

THERE ARE ALTOGETHER 36 DISTRICTS IN PUNJAB. THEY ARE: Attock, Bahawalnagar, Bahawalpur, Bhakkar, Chakwal, Chiniot, Dera Ghazi Khan, Faisalabad, Gujranwala, Gujrat, Hafizabad, Jhang, Jhelum, Kasur, Khanewal, Khushab, Lahore, Layyah, Lodhran, Mandi Bahauddin, Mianwali, Multan, Muzaffargarh, Narowal, Nankana Sahib, Okara, Pakpattan, Rahim Yar Khan, Rajanpur, Rawalpindi, Sahiwal, Sargodha, Sheikhupura, Sialkot, Toba Tek Singh, Vehari.

There are in all, 29 districts in Sindh. They are: Badin, Dadu, Ghotki, Hyderabad, Jacobabad, Jamshoro, Karachi Central, Kashmore, Khairpur, Larkana, Matiari, Mirpur Khas, Naushahro Firoze, Shaheed Benazir Abad, Qambar Shahdadkot, Sanghar, Shikarpur, Sukkur, Tando Allahyar, Tando Muhammad Khan, Tharparkar, Thatta, Umerkot, Sujawal, Karachi East, Karachi South, Karachi West, Korangi, Malir.

There are a total of 26 districts in KPK. They are: Abbottabad, Bannu, Battagram, Buner, Charsadda, Chitral, Dera Ismail Khan, Hangu, Haripur, Karak, Kohat, Upper Kohistan, Lakki Marwat, Lower Dir, Malakand, Mansehra, Mardan, Nowshera,

Peshawar, Shangla, Swabi, Swat, Tank, Upper Dir, Torghar, Lower Kohistan.

There are in all, 32 districts in Balochistan: Awaran, Barkhan, Kachhi (Bolan), Chagai, Dera Bugti, Gwadar, Harnai, Jafarabad, Jhal Magsi, Kalat, Kech (Turbat), Kharan, Kohlu, Khuzdar, Killa Abdullah, Killa Saifullah, Lasbela, Loralai, Mastung, Musakhel, Nasirabad, Nushki, Panjgur, Pishin, Quetta, Sherani, Sibi, Washuk, Zhob, Ziarat, Lehri, Sohbatpur.

There are in all 13 districts in the tribal areas. They are, Bajaur Agency, Khyber Agency, Kurram Agency, Mohmand Agency, North Waziristan Agency, Orakzai Agency, South Waziristan Agency, FR Bannu, FR Dera Ismail Khan, FR Kohat, FR Lakki Marwat, FR Peshawar, FR Tank.

There are altogether 10 districts in Gilgit Baltistan: They are, Ghanche, Skardu, Astore, Diamer, Ghizer, Gilgit, Hunza, Kharmang, Shigar, Nagar.

There are 10 districts in Azad Jammu and Kashmir. They are: Muzaffarabad, Jhelum valley,Neelum, Mirpur, Bhimber, Kotli, Poonch, Bagh, Haveli, Sudhnati.

The most popular resorts in Pakistan are Nathia Gali, Murree, Kaghan, and Naran. Most tourists, from not only Pakistan but also from other parts of the world visit them and enjoy the natural beauty of these places as well as of the many other scenic areas of Pakistan. In the mountainous region of Sindh, there is a hill station at an altitude of 5000 feet, known as Gorakh Hill. It is a place which Zulfikar Ali Bhutto and Benzair Bhutto visited by helicopter. However, it still lacks the attention it deserves. It is difficult to get to this hill station, but once you get there you find it well worth the effort. Tourism in Pakistan is at a relatively early stage but has the potential to grow into a very important industry.

Epilogue
Evolution of Culture in Pakistan

IN THE FIRST ISSUE OF HIS PERIODICAL *TEHZIBUL IKHLAQ* (1870)
Sir Syed Ahmed wrote:

> The aim of this periodical is to persuade Muslims to perfect their
> culture so that the contempt with which the civilized nations of
> the world regard Muslims is dispelled, and Muslims too become
> known as a respected and civilized nation in the world.

Sir Syed also referred to various intellectuals, such as British
historian Thomas Buckle, according to who climate, soil, food,
and aspects of nature affect intellectual progress in human
beings. Buckle then came to the conclusion that civilization can
progress only in Europe, because the climate of this continent
is pleasant. However, his views conflicted with historical facts,
since the natural environments of the valleys of the Indus, the
Nile, the Tigris, and the Euphrates are vastly different from that
of Europe, yet their civilizations were impressive without doubt.

Pakistan's frontiers today are not what they were in 1947.
Although there seemed to be harmony between East and West
Pakistan at the governmental level, the reality was different.
Instead of strengthening goodwill, attempts were made to

concentrate resources and power in West Pakistan. No session of the National Assembly was held in Dhaka. Few Bengalis were recruited in the Pakistan Army with the excuse that they were not as well-built as the West Pakistani races. Most of the income from the export of jute, beetle nut, beetle leaf, tea and Bengali handicrafts was spent on development in West Pakistan.

The traditional attire of East Pakistani women was the sari, though women from Christian and Parsi families as well as Muslims from Bihar, and sometimes even from other parts of India also frequently wore saris. There were attempts to lessen the growing distance between speakers of Urdu and Bengali by translating Bengali into Urdu and vice versa, but wounds had run deep. Aided and abetted by Indian forces, East Pakistanis went to war with West Pakistanis, and in the end the Pakistani army had to surrender to their Indian counterparts. Subsequently, 93,000 civilians and personnel from the Pakistan Army were taken to India where they remained imprisoned for two years. East Pakistan became Bangladesh, and the new country adopted Tagore's poem Sonar Bangla as their national anthem.

Pakistan today is a state in which people of every province have their own identity. The Baloch headgear or pagri has six yards of cloth so does the shalwar worn by Baloch men. This abundance of fabric in the Baloch attire is explained by the intense heat of Baloch summers, which the many folds of fabric help to mitigate.

There are many 'Khans' in Balochistan, each of whom is the chief of a particular area, for example the Khan of Kalat. The

Khan's orders are obeyed and his rules prevail even in the presence of local and provincial administration.

The rangers and army get rid of the terrorists, make highways, and in addition are responsible for guarding the construction of the super highway being built with the help of China, which is spread all over Pakistan.

Baloch women now work in offices, schools, and colleges. Several are even employed in airports. In Balochistan, Balochi, Brahvi, and Pashto speaking people live separately as communities, just as in America Blacks, Chinese and Latinos live in their own communities. No provision is yet in place to educate children in the Balochi, Brahvi, and Pashto languages even at the primary level.

The traditional culture offers two modes of settlement in a quarrel between two tribes:

1. The smaller tribe sends its women with their heads uncovered to the bigger tribe. To indicate their acceptance of the peace overture the bigger tribe covers the heads of the women with chadors.

2. Or, an elderly man in the larger tribe marries a young girl from the smaller tribe, as another way of settling a dispute between two tribes. This kind of marriage, between and elderly male and (usually) a child is prohibited by law. However, tradition keeps the practice alive.

A similar custom known as *vani* or *sawara* still prevails in Khyber Pakhtunkhwa. Pakistan is a country where the history of civilization goes back seven thousand years. Influences of many cultures can be found in this land: The great civilizations of the Indus valley, Mohenjo-Daro and Harappa, the Buddhist Gandhara civilization, and the Muslim civilization terminating in the Mughal culture, as well as other influences such as those of the British. In addition to all the moral, religious, and cultural influences provided by the different eras, were customs and rituals of neighbouring countries like Iran, Afghanistan, and the central Asian countries, which left their effect on customs of various groups in the country. Religion of course contributes its own hue to culture, however it does not fuse different cultures, because if it did there would be no difference between cultures of Muslim communities and countries all over the world. This is why when people wish to turn Pakistani culture into Arab culture, it shows that they have not given due recognition to the rights of geographical and local factors.

Whether it is Sind, Punjab, or Fata, the different styles of chadors the women wear there is part of their identity, just as the area-specific kameez and shalwar worn by men is a sign of their identity.

At one time roti-making plants were established in Pakistan, in order to reduce the drudgery of making bread every day, for Pakistani women. However, these plants could not change the custom of women making roti for the household, and fizzled out.

In Pakistani households food is usually eaten with one's fingers. However, in large functions now spoons and forks are used in imitation of the West. In the days of the 'One unit', an attempt was made to impose a single culture over the whole region. But it had the opposite effect, and we witnessed the emergence of a movement to protect local culture, language, and literature. Prose and poetry writing in Siraiki, Sindi, Balochi, Brahvi, Punjabi, Kashmiri, and Gilgiti was given a fillip, but Urdu's status as the lead national language remained unchanged.

In the matter of dress, though suits and ties are worn to work, and formal occasions, but in traditional functions like weddings, attractive local attire is the first preference.

Local native food has also regained its position as the hot favourite. The Baloch *sajji*, Peshawar's *chapli kabab*, Sindhi biryani and *palla* fish, *kulchas*, *baqar khanis* and *shab degh* from Kashmir, Karachi's *sheermals*, and *nihari*, *paayae*, and *haleem* from Lahore, apricot murabba from Gilgit, and even *qulfa falooda*—all have their demand in every corner of the country.

Now, though everybody speaks their own particular language or dialect, Urdu is the language of communication not only in every corner of the country, but also in every part of the world where Pakistanis live.

The media has promoted the literature of our languages and our tastes. Now that the world is a global village the culture of Pakistan is absorbing, in addition to English, words from other languages as well as tastes from other countries. The Afghani *naan* and Indian thali were already popular; but people now also enjoy shawarma, and the Japanese sushi. Bread made of corn flour with saag is now relished in winter in many parts of the world.

In the subcontinent, weather affects cooking, songs, games, crafts and flowers. People enjoy the fragrance of earth soaked by the first rain of the season—an enjoyment that has found its way into literature and local music. Men and women working in the fields turn on their radios not only to listen to songs but also BBC news.

Copying branded designs, and CDs of movies, music, or favorite TV plays is so widespread and done with such impunity that this practice seems to have become part of our culture too!

The only thing we seem to lack is education and critical thinking. Children are taught to read the Quran, but whether it is a madrasa, a tutor who comes to the house, or one's mother or elderly relative who teaches the children in the family, few seem to attach any importance to teaching students to read the meaning of the Arabic text. The young men of today ride motorbikes. The elderly make do with bicycles.

The culture of Pakistan is linked to our soil which is covered in places by sand and in places by gravel. In other places there are streams, on one shore of which a woman can be seen filling her mud vessel with water while on the other shore, buffaloes slake their thirst. Bottles filled with the same water, though in the Western style, are presented to us to drink. These are pages in the book of culture. You will find, here, the golden shower and, there, buds of *kachnar* and jasmine. People are happy when monsoon rains fall on fragrant soil. This is our culture, and this our civilization.